A U-Turn on the Road to Serfdom

First published in Great Britain in 2014 by
The Institute of Economic Affairs
2 Lord North Street
Westminster
London SW1P 3LB
in association with London Publishing Partnership Ltd
www.londonpublishingpartnership.co.uk

The mission of the Institute of Economic Affairs is to improve public understanding of the fundamental institutions of a free society, with particular reference to the role of markets in solving economic and social problems.

Copyright © The Institute of Economic Affairs 2014

The moral right of the author has been asserted.

A CIP catalogue record for this book is available from the British Library.

ISBN 978-0-255-36686-1

Many IEA publications are translated into languages other than English or are reprinted. Permission to translate or to reprint should be sought from the Director General at the address above.

Typeset in Kepler by T&T Productions Ltd
www.tandtproductions.com

Printed and bound in Great Britain by Page Bros

CONTENTS

THE AUTHORS

Grover Norquist

Grover Glenn Norquist is the founder and president of Americans for Tax Reform. He is the creator and organiser of the Taxpayer Protection Pledge, a public written commitment to oppose all tax hikes, signed by most members of the US Congress. Norquist is a graduate of Harvard College and Harvard Business School. He also serves on the board of directors of the Center for the National Interest, the Parental Rights Organization and the National Rifle Association.

Nima Sanandaji

Nima Sanandaji is a Swedish author of Kurdish origin who holds a PhD from the Royal Institute of Technology in Stockholm. He has written books and reports about policy issues such as women's career opportunities, integration, entrepreneurship and reforms which encourage innovation in the provision of public services.

Matthew Sinclair

Matthew Sinclair is a senior consultant at Europe Economics – a consultancy specialising in economic regulation, competition policy and the application of economics to public policy and business issues – and a former chief executive of the TaxPayers' Alliance. He was the editor of the book *How to Cut Public Spending* (2010) and author of *Let Them Eat Carbon: The Price of Failing Climate Change Policies and How Governments and Big Business Profit from Them* (2011).

David B. Smith

David B. Smith studied at Trinity College, Cambridge, and the University of Essex in the 1960s. He then worked as an economist, predominantly in banks and the securities industry, until the mid 2000s. David is currently a visiting professor at the University of Derby and maintains his own econometric forecasting model of the international and UK economies at Beacon Economic Forecasting. He has written extensively on monetary policy and financial regulation as well as on public spending and tax issues.

FOREWORD

The IEA was honoured to host Grover Norquist, president of Americans for Tax Reform, for the 2014 Hayek Memorial Lecture. Norquist took as one of his main themes the observation that we are on the road to serfdom, as predicted by Hayek in his book *The Road to Serfdom*. Norquist laid out an action plan, grounded in political economy, to suggest how the US could do a U-turn and return to being a low tax and low regulation economy.

Grover Norquist expressed optimism that the tide could be turned in the US. There were a number of reasons for this. Firstly, there is a large coalition of people with different priorities but who believe that the state should 'leave them alone'. There is little in common, for example, between those who wish to have the right to bear arms, those who home-school their children and those who are trying to start small businesses. However, they all wish to be left alone by government to pursue their different interests and their well-being. At the same time, the coalition of people who wish to increase the power of government is becoming harder to hold together. Secondly, in the US, there is a well-thought-out plan – the Ryan plan – for reducing government spending at the federal level to more sustainable levels. There is also competition between states. States – many of them in severe financial trouble as a result of high spending, low economic growth and large future pension commitments – have an incentive to reduce taxes and regulation to attract business.

The future of the US economy is certainly relevant to the UK. However, not all the analysis of our Hayek lecturer could be applied directly to the UK's political and economic situation at the present time. It is necessary to draw lessons from the analysis in order to create the sort of momentum that Grover Norquist described in the US. For that reason, we asked three economists to comment on the lecture and provide some further European context.

In his chapter, David B. Smith discusses the empirical evidence that shows just how far we have moved down the road to serfdom. In countries such as the UK, the government is spending about as much as the people. A peacetime economy is being run with war-time levels of government spending. The levels of taxation necessary to finance government spending also have a serious impact on economic growth. In order to effect the change discussed by Grover Norquist, it is necessary to educate opinion formers about the damage done by current policies.

Matthew Sinclair's commentary deals with the important issue of fiscal decentralisation. In the UK we have one of the world's most centralised taxation systems which contrasts starkly with the situation in the US. As Matthew Sinclair explains, this not only makes it more difficult to reduce the size of the state, it also leads to less efficient service provision. Sinclair details a plan to take the UK system of local government finance closer to that in the US.

Finally, Nima Sanandaji develops Grover Norquist's observation that it is necessary to build a coalition of people who have a strong belief in – and interest in – economic freedom. Drawing on his experience of Sweden, Sanandaji shows how radical reform can create interest groups that wish to promote further reform as well as wish to protect the reforms that have already happened. Sanandaji has two other observations. The first is that entrepreneurial activity can undermine entrenched government interests in unexpected ways. The second is that taxes should be made as visible as possible so that people understand the true costs of government spending.

The 2013 Hayek lecture, together with the commentaries, form an important contribution to the discussion of the role of government in economic life. As government spending and taxation have increased in recent years, it is important to discuss both the economic consequences of this and the political economy mechanisms that might lead to a change in policy. As such, the IEA commends this collection.

PHILIP BOOTH
Editorial and Programme Director
Institute of Economic Affairs
Professor of Insurance and Risk Management
Cass Business School, City University
March 2014

The views expressed in this monograph are, as in all IEA publications, those of the author and not those of the Institute (which has no corporate view), its managing trustees, Academic Advisory Council members or senior staff.

ACKNOWLEDGEMENTS

The Institute of Economic Affairs would like to thank CQS for its very generous sponsorship of the 2013 Hayek Memorial Lecture and of this publication.

SUMMARY

- There is a growing coalition of people in the US
  who hold a strong view that they would like the
  government to 'leave us alone'. The coalition includes
  home-schoolers, those who run small businesses and
  taxpayers. These groups do not want special favours
  from government and their priorities are very different
  from each other. However, the coalition is united in its
  desire for the government not to interfere in their lives.
- There is a coalition opposed to the 'leave us alone'
  coalition. This is the 'takings coalition' that views
  the proper role of government as taking money from
  others and giving it to them. All tax increases feed
  the 'takings coalition' and increase its strength and
  appetite.
- However, if taxes cannot be increased, the interest
  groups that wish to increase spending on their own
  favourite causes will only be able to do so if spending
  is decreased on other programmes – choices will have
  to be made and the 'takings coalition' will become
  fractious.
- Because there is a significant degree of fiscal
  decentralisation in the US, the states can lead the
  way in reducing government spending, taxation and
  regulation.

- In the US, states can copy each other's successful policies. States are, in a sense, in competition with each other. Those that follow policies that discourage business will see an exodus to states that have lower taxes and regulatory burdens. This is already happening.
- Currently, a majority of people live in states that have governors and legislatures that would be sympathetic to an agenda of lower taxation and less regulation. This provides reason for optimism.
- At the federal level, the Ryan budget plan provides hope that there will be a significant reduction in government spending compared with current projections. The plan would lead to lower and simpler taxes and the decentralisation of responsibility for welfare programmes. Ponzi Medicare and pensions schemes would be replaced by funded, individually controlled, defined contribution plans. If nothing changes in the US, spending at the federal level alone will increase to around 40 per cent of GDP from around 20 per cent today. The Ryan budget plan would bring the spending ratio back down to below 20 per cent.
- In order to maintain – and increase – momentum towards a free economy, we need to create favourable demographic trends. This can be done through radical reforms that give families control over education, pensions and welfare. When such reforms are carried out, those affected will tend to support economic policies that involve a less substantial role for the state.

- Detailed analysis of government spending around the world shows that there have been very rapid increases in the share of national income taken by the government. Since Ronald Reagan's election as president in 1980, the proportion of national income spent by the US government at various levels has increased by around one third to 40 per cent. This increase will have had a significant impact on economic growth. Indeed, if government spending had remained at the same proportion of national income as in 1960, the evidence suggests that national income in the US would now be around 70 per cent higher than its current level.

- There are differences between European countries and the US. In particular, the UK has a very centralised fiscal system that does not provide the same opportunities for competition as the US federal system. However, there are similarities between Europe and the US when it comes to the dynamics of reform. There are a number of examples in Europe – for example, in health and education reform in Scandinavia – of reform leading to interest groups developing that are averse to reversing policy changes and, indeed, that promote further radical policy change.

TABLES AND FIGURES

1 A U-TURN ON THE ROAD TO SERFDOM: PROSPECTS FOR REDUCING THE SIZE OF THE STATE

Grover Norquist

I am delighted to deliver this year's Hayek lecture. I ran the campaign in the United States to get President George Herbert Walker Bush to award the Presidential Medal of Freedom Award to Friedrich Hayek, and was delighted when that happened in 1992. Friedrich Hayek wrote *The Road to Serfdom* describing both the forces that drove the growth of government and the dangers of socialism by any name. Hayek argued in 1944 that it was not just a German problem, it was our problem as well. He predicted the future too well – the recent past we have lived.

Margaret Thatcher promised 'no U-turn' in her drive to limit government. What I want to talk about today is this: how do we execute a U-turn and reverse direction on our present road to serfdom here in Britain, in the United States and throughout the world? In the United States, in 1774, when we were still a colony, the government spent 2 per cent of the American colonists' income. At the same time, the nice people of London had 20 per cent of their income taken in taxes. Over the last several centuries, things have become rougher on both sides of the Atlantic as far as liberty is concerned. The state has grown. In the United States a third of people's income, on average, goes to the government, and here it has grown as well. How do we turn this around? How do we get from heading in the wrong direction, decade after decade, in terms of the size and scope of government, and begin to move towards more limited government?

In the United States, one of the first things that was important was to get the political parties aligned in a way that made sense. We have two parties in the United States. In Europe, a party can get 2 per cent of the vote in some countries and it can then decide who the prime minister is and be very important. In the United States, if you get 2 per cent of the vote in an election, you're officially a 'nut'. You may get to be a radio talk show host after the election, but you don't fly in the big aeroplane, and you don't get to serve in Congress. So we divide up into two teams. For many decades, the two teams, the Republicans and Democrats, were largely regional parties.

If somebody told you they were Republican, the only thing you knew about them was that they were born north of the Mason–Dixon Line. You didn't know if they wanted a bigger government or a smaller government – or anything else. There were conservatives who were Democrats, and liberals[1] who were Republicans. There were quite a number of little old ladies in Mississippi who agreed with Ronald Reagan on absolutely everything and voted for George McGovern, because Sherman had recently been quite unpleasant to Atlanta.

---

1   Editor's note: this refers to 'liberals' in the US sense of the word.

The 'leave us alone' coalition

During Reagan's lifetime, we did sort out the two parties along lines of principle not geography. One party largely supports reducing the size and scope of the state and increasing individual liberty. The other party tends to see human progress requiring an increasingly powerful and large government. The central issue dividing the parties is the size of the state. The Republican Party today, the Reagan Republican Party, is a collection of individuals with one thing in common: on the issue that moves their vote – not every issue, but on the issue that moves their vote – what they want from the government is simply to be left alone.

Who sits at the Republican table? Taxpayers, people who vote on the tax issue. They want the tax burden reduced. People concerned about property rights want their property rights respected. The business community – big businesses and small businesses – are not asking for special favours: they are not asking for the government to go and kneecap competitors, they just wish to be left alone (there are businesses that want the government to go and kneecap their competitors, but they bat for the other team). Around this table are also two million Americans who home-school their children. This freedom was only legalised in the past 25 years. These are people making tremendous sacrifices to give their children an education. It is a major commitment and the dominant issue in their life. They do not knock on your door and tell you that you should be a home-schooler: they simply wish to be left alone. The millions of Americans who make the sacrifice to pay for private and parochial education for their children – in addition to their taxes – also hold parental rights in education as a vote-moving political principle.

Then there is the Second Amendment community – I fully realise that nobody in Europe understands this but, in the United States, the Second Amendment, or gun rights, is a big issue. More than nine million Americans have a concealed-carry permit allowing them to carry a gun on their person. Almost twenty million Americans have hunting licences. I serve on the board of directors for the National Rifle Association, which has four million members. We don't go around urging people to be hunters. We don't require that all fourth-grade children be taught books in state schools entitled 'Heather has Two Hunters'. We are simply asking to be left alone to protect ourselves and our families.

There are also members of the various communities of faith in the United States for whom the most important thing in their life is to practise their faith and to transmit it to their children. Evangelical Christians, Roman Catholics, Orthodox Jews, Muslims and Mormons hold very different views of religion, but are united in their preferred relationship with the state: they simply want to be left alone. For each group, first choice, when we were designing the Constitution, might have been: 'make everybody be my religion', but because we were already diverse at the beginning, the achievable second choice was 'everybody gets left alone'.

This is an extremely important thing to understand because, sometimes when you hear the discussion in the

United States, you would think that the coalition I am describing will not hold together because some of the 'religious right' want to impose their religious values on others. That is why you have to look at political activity in terms of vote-moving issues. The 'religious right' came into being in the 1970s. Why? It was because the Carter administration was going after Christian radio stations, using the 'fairness doctrine', a regulation originally designed to require TV and radio news to present both sides of a political issue. Christian radio viewed this as an assault on religious liberty. In addition, the Internal Revenue Service (IRS) was threatening to revoke the non-profit status of Christian schools, which were seen by the government-school teachers' unions as a competitive threat: so these groups organised in self-defence; they wanted to be left alone; they feared state power. Understand that and you will understand why they sit at the same table and work reasonably well with people who work all day, never go to church, and simply want to pay lower taxes.

What is important is that everyone around the table wishes to be left alone on their key issue, and they vote for the same candidate. The candidate says, 'I will leave your kids alone, your guns alone, your money alone, your property alone, your faith alone' and he wins the votes of all these people.

Then the candidate and the party that puts itself in that position can move forward. It doesn't mean everyone in the centre-right coalition agrees on everything: they certainly don't. They don't all have tea together; they don't socialise. The guy who wants to make money all day looks across the table at the guy who wants to go to church all day and says, 'That's not how I spend my time.' They both look over at the guy who wants to fondle his guns all day and say: 'That's not how we spend our time.' But, for the party of liberty to advance, it is not necessary that everyone is agreed on what they would do with their liberty. It is simply necessary that we each agree on moving towards liberty.

That's how the coalition became self-aware in time for the 1980 election. The establishment looked at it and said, 'This will fall apart any moment,' because they were looking at the secondary and tertiary issues on which the coalition did not agree. There you will find lots of disagreements, but on primary vote-moving issues, they are not in conflict.

Conflict among the opponents of liberty: the 'takings coalition'

When Hillary Clinton was running for the Senate, back in 2000, she gave a speech saying, 'What we progressives need is a meeting like Grover runs in Washington, DC.' I was asked by the press what I thought of that, and I explained how our centre-right coalition meeting works. We put 160 people together every week in a room where there are wide disagreements on what is important, except that what is important to each person is that they be free in the zone that matters to them.

Progressives, the left, have tried to put together similar meetings from time to time. Who would sit at Hillary Clinton's table, recently stolen by Barack Obama? Around the table might be trial lawyers, labour union bosses and big city political machines. Also the two wings of the dependency movement: people who are locked into welfare dependency and people who make $90,000 a year managing the dependency of people and making sure none of them get jobs and become Republicans. Then we have all the coercive utopians: the people who get government grants to push the rest of us around. The people who mandate cars too small to put your entire family into; the people who designed and required that we must all have toilets too small to flush completely; the people who insist on those light bulbs that convince you that you have glaucoma; and the people who require that on the Sabbath you must separate the green glass from the white glass from the brown glass for the recycling priests.

They have a list of things that you have to do and a list of things you are not allowed to do that is slightly longer and more tedious than Leviticus. It just goes on, and on, and on. So around the left's table, the 'takings coalition' can get along with each other as long as there is enough money in the centre of the table. They can work together as long as taxes are raised and there is more money pouring into the centre of the table to share. They can then cheerfully sit together in the way that they do in the movies after the bank robbery passing out the loot: 'One for you, one for you, one for you,' and everybody is happy.

However, if we do our jobs correctly, and we say 'no new taxes' and we stop throwing cash into the centre of that table, then all our friends on the left begin to look at each other in a way that is more like the second-to-last scene in those lifeboat movies. Now they are trying to decide who they are going to eat or who they are going to throw overboard.

Our job, step one in the fight for liberty, is to ensure that we don't make things worse; don't throw money into the centre of the statist table; do not feed the beast. Don't raise taxes is rule number one. If you stop the flow of tax dollars, then the other team, as they see the money pile dwindling, begin gnawing on the guy sitting next to them. If they can't eat taxpayers they will fight each other for the limited amount of other people's money that is available.

The left is not made up of friends and allies; it is made up of competing parasites.

Pledging not to increase taxes

So, how do we strengthen our team? How do we identify more people whose votes and political activities lead towards liberty, and how do we reduce the number of people who view the state as that mechanism whereby they get their hands on other people's stuff, and other people's lives?

Step one, I always thought, was limiting taxation. That is why I run Americans for Tax Reform. We created the Taxpayer Protection Pledge that many candidates sign. It is a written, witnessed pledge to their constituents that they will never vote to raise taxes. The goal of that pledge is to make it difficult for Congress to ever raise taxes because then, and only then, can you begin to have a conversation about reducing spending. Once you remove the tax hike option then you may have an opportunity to focus on reforming government to cost less.

We learned the importance of holding the line against taxes in two painful failures by Republican presidents Reagan and Bush 41. In 1982, the Democrat party said to Reagan: 'We promise to cut spending by three dollars if you agree to raise taxes by one dollar.' A three-to-one ratio was agreed. Reagan faced a Democratic House, and a Republican Senate that was pre-Reagan in its thinking. So Reagan was kind of alone. Just as Margaret Thatcher may have been the only Thatcherite in her own government at first, Reagan was the only Reaganite in Washington for quite some time. He took that bad deal. At the end of the day, taxes were raised and spending was not reduced.

This happened eight years later, to George Bush senior. They offered him two dollars of imaginary spending cuts for every dollar of tax increases. Spending didn't get cut but taxes did get raised. The other team raises taxes to spend the money; they don't raise taxes for some other purpose, so if you give them the tax increases, they will spend the resources.

In 1994, Republicans won majorities in the House and Senate and all but a handful signed and kept the pledge to never raise taxes. Republicans learned from painful failure that tax hikes only feed big government and strengthen the party of big government in the United States: the Democrats.

So the Reagan Republican Party became the party that would never raise your taxes. But opposing tax increases is a necessary but not sufficient condition to achieve limited government.

Reducing spending

The second step is to stop spending so much money. One of the failures of George W. Bush's eight years as president was that he was very good at not raising taxes – but not so good at restraining spending. He had learned the dangers of tax hikes. Bush 43 watched dad raise taxes and lose his bid for re-election in 1992. Dad had been a great president on many things; he managed the collapse of the Soviet Union without a lot of blood on the floor, and kicked Iraq out of Kuwait without getting stuck occupying the place for a decade. There was one problem: he raised taxes. And he threw away a perfectly good presidency as a result.

We did begin to make progress in limiting government spending in 2011. What changed was the arrival of the Tea Party movement. This was a radical change in American politics. It has completed the circle in terms of who sits around the centre-right's 'leave us alone' table.

Before the Tea Party revolt beginning in 2009, most Americans believed that you could not win elections by attacking government overspending. But Americans would organise opposition and win elections once 'spend too much' became 'tax too much'. That was the lesson of the 1978 taxpayer victory of Proposition 13 designed to cut property taxes in California. The California tax increases in the late 1970s were the product of overspending, but the revolt followed the tax hikes not the earlier overspending. Reagan ran for president promising to cut federal spending by $90 billion in 1976 and lost a Republican primary.

He won in 1980 and 1984 as the tax cutter. QED. Americans hated tax hikes but not necessarily government spending.

In January 2009, Obama came into power. Within two and a half months, he had threatened to spend trillions – the stimulus and more. The whole point of the stimulus package was to take over $800 billion dollars and throw it in the middle of the 'takings coalition' table to keep everybody happy.

This scared Americans, and we had about a million Americans in the streets demonstrating at between 600 and 800 rallies around the United States on the week of 15 April. This was unprecedented. These were not unemployed students. These were men and women with jobs, lives, families. They had never been in a demonstration. And they were not reacting to tax increases – those were yet to come. They were organising in opposition to government spending.

There have been some very good studies about how this affected the voter turnout in places where you had rallies compared with places where they planned a rally, but it rained, so it was cancelled. You could see that we gained between three million and six million voters in 2010 because of increased political activism: the idea of showing up, seeing other people, realising you weren't alone and that you weren't crazy was very important.

This was all part of fighting against 'spend too much'. In November 2010, we elected a great number of people largely on the anti-spending issue. To 'no new taxes' the movement added 'and stop spending so much'. We now have a more internally consistent Reagan Republicanism that opposes tax hikes and spending demands: a focus on reducing spending that buttresses and complements the other 'leave us alone' issues.

So, in 2011, when we had the argument between the Republicans in the House and Obama over the debt ceiling increase we were confident we had popular support. We held fast and won. The final agreement did not raise taxes as the Democrats had demanded. Instead we won $2.5 trillion in spending restraint: cuts from planned spending over the decade with real budget caps and a sequester protecting those budget savings.

The Ryan budget

Just as the Tea Party demonstrations in 2009 and the Republican capture of the House of Representatives in November 2010 demonstrated real political muscle in the anti-spending movement, Congressman Paul Ryan of Wisconsin introduced his Path to Prosperity budget for the United States. Potentially, this is the U-turn on the road to serfdom. The Ryan plan combines tax reform and spending reform. Ryan's tax reform lowers corporate and individual marginal tax rates down to 25 per cent and moves the United States to a territorial tax system so that we don't double tax expatriates who live overseas and businesses that are doing business overseas. It also moves towards full expensing for business investment. The plan would be very pro-growth and it greatly simplifies the tax code and makes it more transparent.

On the spending side, Ryan takes many of the 185 means-tested welfare programmes and would provide block grants to the 50 states. States would, over time, receive less in federal aid in return for more freedom to run their programmes. When this was done with AFDC – the aid to families with dependent children programme – in 1996, the states dramatically reduced welfare spending and many poor Americans were freed from welfare dependency. We reformed welfare and saved money by giving states more autonomy. The Ryan plan proposes this for the other major welfare programmes. Ryan also proposes reforms to underfunded entitlement programmes, such as Medicare, to eliminate unfunded liabilities.

Without such reforms, government spending on entitlements will drive total federal spending from 20 per cent of GDP to as high as 40 per cent of GDP. The Ryan plan reforms government to cost less and lowers federal government spending down to somewhere below 20 per cent of GDP.

So the Ryan plan would take government to about half of what it would otherwise be. But turning a ship round takes a long time. The reforms in this plan would be phased in slowly, minimising opposition. The Republican Party is united in support of the Ryan plan. One or two people voted no because they thought it wasn't tough enough. But almost every Republican Congressman and Senator supported the budget, voted for it, and they got re-elected in 2012.

They have now voted for it three times. There is a depth of understanding within the modern Republican Party of what this plan does. When I was first speaking with Congressman Ryan about his plan, I asked, 'Do you want me to help to get co-sponsors?' Normally, a congressman wishes to have many co-sponsors to show support and strength. Instead Ryan said, and I paraphrase, 'No, I'm not going to let anyone co-sponsor the Ryan budget plan until I am convinced they understand it, so that when they talk to the press, they articulate it correctly; they don't misstate what's in it or say things that might come back to hurt the plan. I want them to be serious advocates and apostles for the plan.' And he did that.

Again, early in 2013, I called Congressman Ryan and said: 'You know, Hernando De Soto would like to come by and visit you to talk about some of the work he's doing on property rights in Tunisia and some other countries.' Ryan said: 'Oh, that would be great. I'm a big fan of his work. Let's get together in two and a half months.' I said, 'That long? He just needs half an hour.' Congressman Ryan said: 'At the moment, I am meeting with every member of the Republican caucus to work through this budget; the update of the last one, so that they have a full understanding of what is in the budget.' He is talking in detail about the changes from last year to this year. That is the depth of knowledge about the plan. So, when we talk about Republicans taking the Senate and the presidency we know what they will do.

This is not wishful thinking. The Republican vision for saving the economy and American liberty is the Ryan plan. It is written down. Every member of Congress gets yelled at about it by folks from the left; they get asked about it by the press. They can competently defend it and articulate it, which I think is extremely important.

The role of inter-state competition in widening the 'leave us alone' coalition

So that's the national level; that's the future in the United States. We are on the road to serfdom. We do the U-turn when we have a Republican majority in the House of Representatives and a Republican Senate – where we need just 51 votes to cut spending, not 60 – and a Republican president to sign the bills.

When and how do we do that? There are 25 red states with a Republican governor, Republican House and Republican Senate: 165 million Americans live in states with complete Republican control of the state government. This, by the way, is after the 2012 election, when, if you read *The New York Times*, the modern Republican Party ceased to exist. Then there are 13 states where the Democrats have complete control: California, Illinois and Vermont, for example. They have 81 million people.

So a quarter of the country lives in Democrat states; more than half in Republican states, and the rest have split governance between the governorship, House and Senate at state level. These are the people who redistricted congress between 2010 and 2012. So every 10 years, we redraw the lines both at the state legislative level and in Congress. When you look at who controls state legislatures, the states which have Republican legislatures voted to write the rules for the next ten years to keep themselves in power and the Democrat states did the same thing there. So these states are going to be pretty much the same for around ten years.

You have got 25 basically Republican states and 13 Democrat states, and they are moving in dramatically different directions. Just in the last two years, you see the Democrat states raising taxes so as to not have to reform state pensions. On the other hand, you are seeing Republican states such as Utah reform their state pension system. In Utah, starting a year ago, everybody who is hired as a teacher, policeman, state worker, county, local government worker and so on will have a 401(k) pension plan – an individual retirement account rather than the promise of an unfunded state pension from the government. Utah says: 'Here is your pay; here is 10 per cent of your pay that goes into your individual savings account. That is our full contribution to your pension.' This is how we end the creation of unfunded liabilities. Other red states are following Utah in moving to a defined contribution model and away from a defined benefit system that leads to politically driven overpromising. In Democrat Illinois and California they decided to raise taxes instead of undertake reforms.

Changing the demographics

For the next ten years America will have a Republican House thanks to the marvels of redistricting. They have a good shot at winning the Senate over the next several election cycles and we have two presidential elections: 2016 and 2020. I believe that the Republicans will capture the

Senate and the presidency either in 2016 or in 2020. Then the Ryan plan will be implemented and we will have done the U-turn on the road to serfdom, and we will be heading in the right direction again. To turn us back, the Democrats would have to take everything and hold it for a while, which I think unlikely.

Now, what do we do? Do we just sit and wait for victory to arrive? No, and that is where the progress at the state level is very important. There has been a lot of discussion about demographic changes in the United States. When Democrats talk about demographics, they just mean race and ethnicity. They are not thinking about vote-moving issues. They think everybody is voting and always will vote based on their race and ethnicity. When Bertolt Brecht, the left-of-centre playwright, was trying to explain what happened in 1953 when the East German workers were revolting against the party of the workers (the Communists) he announced that what they needed to do in East Germany was elect a new people. It couldn't be the government's fault; we needed new people.

Well, in point of fact, we can elect a new people. You elect a new people by changing laws to move people from the 'takings coalition' that has an interest in expanding the state and helping them see that their interests lie in the 'leave us alone' coalition. Where that is happening now, and will continue to happen over the next few decades, is at the state level. I will give you a few examples, starting with the laws that allow home-schooling.

There are two million parents who home-school. Those people are solidly pro-freedom. The government has offered to help babysit their kids for free for 12 years, and they have said, 'Thanks, but we'll do it.' Not only are they winning all of the spelling bees as a result of home-schooling, they are a highly active and aware part of the movement for liberty. Only 30 years ago the government was putting people in prison for home-schooling: it was illegal in all states. That has now been changed.

The voucher movement – the school choice movement – is also important. We now have three states that have dramatically increased the number of vouchers or scholarships available for lower-income students to attend government, private or parochial schools. Today there are 300,000 people eligible for a $5,000 voucher in Arizona alone, 500,000 in Indiana and 500,000 in Louisiana.

So you now have a mass voucher experiment for parents who are told: 'Here is a $5,000 scholarship for your child each year.' I particularly like Arizona because the deal is: 'Here is your $5,000. If you only spend $4,000, you can put the $1,000 into an education savings account, which you can use in future years and which accumulates and grows as you move forward.' So a parent has $5,000 dollars, per child, and they walk around and say to the local government school: 'Here's what I'm interested in, and if you meet my child's needs you get the $5,000 or I could take that $5,000 to a private school or a charter school, or I could home-school and I get to keep the money.'

All of a sudden, they have the attention of the government school system, as well as of the private schools that exist already, and others that are being created. You have a different human being when they carry that kind of power with them. Before, if you were to complain to the government school, they told you to go away. They considered parents an annoyance. This changes with a voucher or scholarship system and this also changes the nature of the person who carries the voucher.

The Second Amendment issue is also important. In the United States, as I have noted, we now have 4 million members of the National Rifle Association. We have about 18 million hunters, but every year there are fewer hunters. It is dropping by as much as 25 per cent each generation as there is just less land near cities for people to do bird hunting. That number is going down.

However, starting in the 1980s, we began to pass concealed-carry laws. This means that, if you are 21 years old and have not been convicted of any offence recently, you can be issued with a concealed-carry permit to carry a gun: in your purse, in your car or on your person.

Over 40 states have these laws. I am from Massachusetts. We have more restrictions – what is known as a 'may issue' rather than 'shall issue' law. If the mayor likes you, or the police chief likes you, he may give you a permit. In 40 states, they have to give you the permit. So, 9.3 million Americans now have concealed-carry permits. People who have such permits are different people from those who say: 'Gee, if I get in trouble, the nice policeman will come and draw a chalk line around me. That will be helpful.' Instead, they say: 'No, I'm in charge of this part of my life.'

Another factor is the number of government workers. If you are a government worker in the United States for 30 years, you are 30 per cent more likely to be a Democrat.

Regardless of all other demographics, over time working for the government changes people's politics – government workers tend to vote for bigger government.

The good news is that, as you have fewer people working for the state, you improve the prospects for liberty. This is why the number of people who work for the government is an important metric. If you are cutting the size of government you need a strategy and metrics. After the 2001 tax cut, which was in June of the first year of the Bush presidency, the administration did not have a to-do list. As we are working on expanding liberty, we need to have a to-do list.

What will we do when crises happen, so we can, as the saying goes, never let a good crisis go to waste? Well, every time there was a crisis in the Bush administration, the left came up and said: 'You've got to spend more money; you've got to have more regulations.' If you don't have a plan you will implement the plan the other team has prepared.

So when Enron went bankrupt, New Orleans was flooded or Fannie Mae and Freddie Mac lost money – indeed, whenever there was a crisis – the response was to call for more government. The crisis was never presented as a reason for less government, or reforming government: it was always a good argument for more of the same policies that created the crisis.

We learned from the Bush administration that, if you do not go in with a plan of what you want to do, you fail. This is why the Ryan plan is so important – it is written down; it is internalised. An entire political party has signed up to it. If you do not do that, you just get pushed into bigger government by every 'crisis'.

So, you can change demographics. When we came up with concealed-carry laws, we changed the nature of nine million people to make them more freedom-loving. Home-schooling did the same for two million people: it became a vote-moving issue for them. More people – about half of Americans – have 401(k) individual retirement accounts. That is a number that is growing. If you live in the United States and you have $5,000 in a personal savings account or retirement savings account, it makes you 18 per cent more Republican and less Democrat, on average. All demographic groups: white, black, old, young, rich, poor, government worker, private-sector worker become more Republican with share ownership – direct share ownership.

For this reason, the Republican solution to many problems has a common element: education savings accounts, health savings accounts, retirement savings accounts, individual retirement accounts, lifetime savings accounts, and so on. This is because, if people are investing in the stock market and saving for the future, and they see this investment growing over time, then their politics change. That is why Bush wanted to privatise Social Security, though he did not have enough votes in the Senate. His goal was to privatise Social Security so that every 18-year-old would look ahead to having hundreds of thousands of dollars in a bank account. Even if they had a low-paying job all through their career, they could accumulate wealth and that would change the nature of who they are.

So we can create a new electorate; we can change demographics. Not all demographics are based on gender, race, ethnicity and religion. In fact the issues I am talking about are all legislated at the state level and you are seeing this effort state by state. The Democrats are trying to put more people on government payrolls in blue states. Republicans are trying to have fewer people on government payrolls. Democrats are not interested in people owning defined contribution pensions whereas the Republican states are very interested. So far, we have only seen two years of 25 Republican states going in one direction and 13 Democrat states going in the other. Every Republican state can, if it wishes, turn itself into Texas or Hong Kong as rapidly as it wants to. Every Democrat state can turn itself into California or Greece as rapidly as it wants to.

The country is moving in two dramatically different directions, in such a way that you can see the comparison. Compare Indiana and Illinois: Indiana is red state; Illinois is blue state. Indiana has just passed a right-to-work law, which says that nobody can be forced to join a union (22 states now have such laws). Indiana is one of the first heavily industrialised eastern states that did so. It is cutting taxes; it is pursuing school choice. Across the border, in Illinois, they are raising taxes; they are giving the unions more power. On that border, how many factories will be built on the western (Illinois) side in the next 20 years? There are going to be very real consequences because some states are doing it right and some states are performing poorly.

You may have read in the newspaper that President Obama has an interest in collecting data on certain individuals throughout the world. In his administration, there has, though, been an effort to stop collecting one particular piece of information: they have announced that they are going to stop keeping track of how many people move and how much income moves from one state to another. They were calculating every year, for example, how many people have left California in the previous 20 years (it was more than a million). When you raise taxes in California, and middle-income people flee the state, you can actually calculate how much taxable income leaves. They had a millionaire's tax in Maryland, and the following year they went to count the millionaires, and there were fewer than there were before.

The Obama administration is not interested in having people see those numbers and it was going to try to stop them being produced. But these data are exactly what helps make the case for more liberty as we move forward because we have competition between states.

This is federalism. We have 50 states and we want the 50 states to compete to provide the best and most competent government at the lowest cost, to attract people and capital and jobs. And we can keep score. Americans love to keep score. We talk about loser states; nothing bothers governors more than when I refer to loser states. The government is trying to figure out how to tax across state lines on the Internet, because it wants to be able to reach out from loser states and grab hold of some of the cash of the citizens who have been fleeing those states.

As we move forward, another issue is that of union dues. This is important in terms of changing the electorate. Governor Scott Walker of Wisconsin changed the law and said that if you are a government worker the government is not going to take money out of your pay packets for union dues. The average teacher who's paid $50,000 in Wisconsin was paying $1,000 in dues and it used to come straight out of the pay packet. If unions want $1,000 from their teachers, they now have to recruit the teachers themselves. What has this done? About a third of the people who used to belong to unions don't belong anymore. There were tens of millions of dollars that used to come from coerced unionisation. Even people who did not wish to be were part of the Democratic Party's political machine, because the unions were sending their money to the Democrat Party and its candidates. We stopped that in Wisconsin.

Other states are looking to do this too. They made a change in Alabama which denies the teachers' unions $14.5 million every four-year cycle. The unions used to get zero-cost fundraising. Those of you who ever do fundraising, imagine zero fundraising costs! You get $1,000 cheques from everybody. You don't have to write them a letter; you don't have to hold events, or buy them anything to drink.

Conclusion

So this is a huge, dramatic change. The fight for liberty in the states is being won. The 'leave us alone' coalition is self-aware. People understand who is in the coalition and why. We step on other people's toes less often because we understand why other people are in the room with us. We understand what motivates the other side, and we have a list of things to do to ensure that the other side shrinks.

If we can get people to join the private sector, get a pension, get a concealed-carry permit law, we can ensure that there are more of us and fewer of them. This moves forward through state legislation at the moment. We will strengthen liberty on a state-by-state basis and then also at the federal level as well.

At the federal level, the forces of liberty have been pushed back over the last 12 years. A lot of money was wasted and a lot of damage has been done. It is not just Obama: the Bush administration was spending too much and wasn't as focused on maximising liberty as it could have been. Bush did not do this on purpose. He started a small fire by mistake. The arsonist is more dangerous: he is doing it on purpose.

First an incompetent fireman and then the dangerous arsonist: that is the challenge we have had. I think we will make the U-turn on the road to serfdom in the United States and that is the project that we are embarking upon. I recommend the idea of competition between states – say in the European Union, or something like that – to reward liberty. States that want to behave like Greece should be punished rather than subsidised. I think that Hayek's vision of the road to serfdom was accurate – all the pressures he talked about, all the things that made that happen. But we do have the opportunity to do a U-turn on the road to serfdom and move back in the correct direction.

2   QUESTIONS AND DISCUSSION

DAVID MYDDELTON: Thank you very much. If it is not too mischievous to point it out, we can't help noticing in London that we get an awful lot of visitors from France these days. I wonder if that says anything about France being a 'loser country'.

STEVEN BAKER MP: I am the Member of Parliament for Wycombe. It is a brilliant, optimistic plan; it is exciting. Will it be interrupted in the chaos that will ensue from QE unwinding?

GROVER NORQUIST: I think we do need to worry very much about the misuse of monetary policy; inflation is a very real danger for all the reasons that the Austrian economists pointed out. It is interesting that Ron Paul was getting young people excited about the Federal Reserve System. So they have actually been getting more people focused on the issue of monetary policy in the United States – and excited about it – than you would have thought humanly possible. When the government controls the money supply inflation is always a danger.

JOHN HINTZE: You talked about the 2016 and 2020 elections. What do you hope the Republican Party learns from the Mitt Romney campaign for those elections?

GROVER NORQUIST: Yes, the presidential races in 2016 and 2020 are our two opportunities to win the presidency. Add the White House to a Republican Congress and we can turn the nation around. So we have got to have a good candidate. We had some challenges in 2012. Firstly, in the 22 debates, we allowed press people – left-of-centre press people – to ask all the questions. That made our candidates look as if they were obsessed with certain issues – abortion, gay marriage, etc. – which were actually the obsession of the guy asking the questions. That was not helpful. Secondly, of the ten people running for president, only three of them were actually running for president. The others were running for radio talk show host, to sell books, undergo marriage counselling, etc. So, we had three guys – the three governors – who were really running for president. Those who were really running for president quit when they lost primaries because they knew they were not going to win. Those who were not really running for president carried on when they lost primaries because they weren't really running for president.

Next time, we will have a much stronger field for a couple of reasons. Firstly, there is a strong group of governors. Governor Walker of Wisconsin, for example. He who took a blue state where they invented public sector unionism, ended compulsory union dues and limited collective bargaining to wages, thereby exempting work rules, pensions, benefits and tenure. Walker cut taxes and expanded school choice dramatically in a traditionally Democrat state. He gained a national following and a national base and he knows all the nice rich people who can write significant cheques.

There is also Governor Rick Perry of Texas, who did not do well in the debates because he was on pain medicine, but who has been one of the best governors in the country for almost 12 years now. He would be a formidable candidate. There is Rand Paul, a senator, though I tend to prefer governors. Rand Paul is a son of Ron Paul and has really been impressing people. He brings an entire 'small-l libertarian' tone and young people's energy into the political spectrum for Republicans. New Jersey Governor Chris Christie cut $130 billion from the state's pension liability. He stopped all tax hike efforts from this Democrat legislature. If the Republican presidential candidate carries New Jersey he wins the presidential election. Christie has governed well and been very impressive. Another candidate is former governor Jeb Bush. He was a reformer and speaks Spanish. He opposed all tax hikes. He probably needs to change his name! There's something unseemly about having Bushes and Clintons. We're always yelling at the guys in North Korea: 'You can't just go from one Kim to the next guy with the same name.' Then we kind of do something that looks too much like that with this back-and-forth between Bushes and Clintons. Louisiana Governor Bobbie Jindal has reformed the state's ethics laws – and they needed it – and expanded school choice, cut taxes and passed tort reform. I don't mean to leave somebody out. There may be seven or eight people who could run seriously, and you would look at them as serious candidates – not as a person who is trying to sell books or be a radio talk show host.

The person who comes out of a field that strong is going to be a strong candidate. With Romney, there was just this sense of unease. People kept looking for somebody other than Romney. We had this serial thing where we would fall in love with some person other than Romney for a short while. Then Romney ultimately won it. But that was not the way to create a strong candidate. Romney had many good assets; he would have been a much better president than Obama, but the situation did not create the strongest candidate.

MALCOLM MATSON: We have long accepted that cartels between commercial and business organisations are not good things. I love your idea of competing states. I am absolutely appalled at how both politically and publicly in this country at the moment there seems to be a fashion for tax cartels, governments getting together to do things which, if done in the commercial arena, would be absolutely appalling. What is the argument that you might give us to show the absurdity and obscenity of that?

GROVER NORQUIST: You are entirely correct. They do it because they don't want tax competition. We citizens want tax competition because we want governments to compete to provide the best government at the lowest cost and not to set up a cartel so they don't have to compete on that basis. The one part of every government that works is the military, because it is the one part that actually deals with competition! They have to be better than the guy next door or the border moves.

So even in countries where nothing works, the army works. What you want is competition not on the military side, but on the basis of competency. People who shrink from competing on the basis of competence are telling you something about their sense of their own abilities. They think they will fail in a competitive world where competent governance is rewarded, and anyone who doesn't want to compete based on competence shouldn't hold that job.

MATTHEW SINCLAIR: I am from the TaxPayers' Alliance. I just wanted to ask you about the current government policy here, which is to have, in their fiscal adjustments, 80 per cent spending cuts and 20 per cent tax hikes. I wonder if you could talk a bit about the politics of these mixed fiscal adjustments, which we are told are the responsible way forward. How do they affect reputations, electoral chances and so on?

GROVER NORQUIST: Yes, raising taxes is what politicians do instead of governing; raising taxes is what politicians do instead of prioritising. If a politician says they are going to raise taxes for education because education is their highest priority, what they have just told you is that actually, education is their lowest priority. Everything else in the budget is more important than a penny more going to education. They are unwilling to spend less on anything else to fund education. So this is very important: if we do not raise taxes, we can have a conversation about reforming government. If tax increases are on the table – we see this in the US all the time – spending cuts never happen.

MIKE HOBDAY: Right at the beginning you said that the first step is to stop raising taxes. I think there is a step before that, which is to build a coalition of like-minded people who want to stop raising taxes, and I think we are very far off that in this country and the rest of Europe, apart from, perhaps, Switzerland, which has been bullied into increasing taxes. Have you got any advice at all for getting to that pre-first step, if you like?

GROVER NORQUIST: Sure: everyone should write a cheque to the TaxPayers' Alliance! Britain is ahead of some other European countries in having a strong, serious taxpayer group. And one of the things that Britain has now is a centre-right meeting: there were 80 or 90 people there when I attended. That is similar to the meetings we have in DC. There are things happening in a number of European countries: France just started a meeting. They had 17 people: they had every single free-market guy in France! Firstly, you want to figure out all the guys who ought to be there, and then build a coalition; structures matter, and learning from each other matters. You have got some good structures here in terms of free-market think-tanks and activist groups. They are communicating with each other.

You then just have to take over a political party, which was a long project for our team in the US.

JOHN MASON: I am an MP in Glasgow. Now, in our country, there has been a lot of publicity about people who hitherto have been hiding their assets in Switzerland, the Channel Islands, the Isle of Man and other tax havens. With effect from this year, they are going to have to pay taxes. So can you tell me a little about what Americans are doing about Americans having money in Switzerland and all these tax havens? If Americans can still hide their assets in these Swiss bank accounts, are they going to have to start paying money on their overseas investments? Can you also say a little about the American government's policy on things like Starbucks, or other big multinational corporations making hundreds of millions, or even billions of pounds of profits, and only paying two or three million in tax?

GROVER NORQUIST: President Obama is pushing very hard to get a tax cartel. Obama is pushing very hard to maintain the worldwide corporate tax system that we have but most of the rest of the world doesn't have. It is because he wants to extend power that way. Because the US government charges additional US tax when profits are repatriated to the US, a great deal of overseas earnings do not come back to the United States. When Bush reduced the extra tax to 4 per cent or so we got about $400 billion back. We could have had a trillion dollars come back under Obama, raising stock prices and making companies and people all that much better off. Obama is so committed to worldwide taxation and not having tax competition that he passed on that opportunity just before his re-election.

They wanted to pierce Swiss banking because of drug money. Well, when you decide to put police on the Internet to look at dirty pictures, or police in banks to look for drug money, the policemen can look for whatever they want. When we passed the Patriot Act, the first person prosecuted was some guy in Las Vegas who ran a strip club. When you give government extra powers for X, it doesn't stay with X. So just watch out: when they want more power for X that is not the end. I remember the Bush people telling me: 'We trust Bush.' I said, 'Yes, but he doesn't get to be president forever. At some point, Hillary Clinton could be president. Do you really want her with these powers?' I think they were short-sighted in the vast expansion of presidential executive powers that we gave our government in DC.

PETER CLARKE: If I had been able to have a séance with Friedrich Hayek's ghost, I think he would have asked me to ask you: what about the state monopoly of the central bank, the currency?

GROVER NORQUIST: We ought not to have one. I think what is interesting is the wonderful project that Ron Paul began called 'audit the Federal Reserve'. It wasn't 'abolish the Federal Reserve', which is what I suspect he really wants to do. He said, 'Let's audit it.' Well, that sounds so terribly reasonable, and then people say they don't want it audited. But then it is a little hard to argue: 'We are not doing anything wrong; there's nothing we are ashamed of. There are no problems we are creating, but please don't look.'

So a whole bunch of people do not want to be transparent; they do not want to be audited. That is ridiculous. I share Ron Paul's sense of where we ought to go in terms of private money versus state monopoly money or, at least for starters, money tied to something of real value.

But the clever way in which he gets us there is to force the other team to defend the indefensible and to engage people who would never engage in this issue because they thought it was too extreme, or not going to happen. He did that by proposing an audit of the Fed. And he got 300 co-sponsors in the House of Representatives for his bill to audit the Fed, including many Democrats.

That was a very helpful step in the right direction and, I think, at the end of the day, we will get there. Once we get the boat turned around, the U-turn on the road to serfdom, there are a number of other projects on which we need to focus as well.

3 THE MODERN LEVIATHAN STATE, ITS GROWTH AND CONSEQUENCES

David B. Smith

In his Hayek lecture, Grover Norquist talked about turning back on the road to serfdom. This chapter considers how far modern states have travelled down that road and examines the consequences in terms of prosperity forgone. The socialisation of the state, about which Grover Norquist talked, preceded the financial crash – and may have partly caused it – but then reached new heights in its wake. It is an open question whether it is possible to turn back. However, it would be enormously beneficial for economic performance and social welfare if we could.

Any attempt to quantify the economic footprint of the state is bedevilled by numerous data difficulties (see Smith 2006). However, the broad trends are sufficiently marked to suggest that the increased role of government was probably the main structural development of the 20th and 21st centuries. This can be seen from Table 1, which uses Tanzi and Schuknecht (2000) for the historical figures, updated using the December 2013 OECD Economic Outlook. Although there are some noticeable inconsistencies between the two sources for individual countries, these appear to be largely offsetting when looking at the average figures for the twelve developed nations for which a continuous record is available (see bottom line).

This average indicates that the 'typical' industrialised state was spending between 10 and 15 per cent of national output before the 1914–18 war (a period that can be regarded as the heyday of genuine free-market capitalism), between a fifth and a third or so in the late 1930s (when Keynes published his *General Theory*), and between one quarter and one third or so in 1960. The mean spending ratio then increased to just over 43 per cent by 1980. This increase was mainly due to the profligate spending policies implemented during the 1960s. This 'big government' era was followed by a move to a lower growth path of national output during the 1970s that resembles developments since 2008. Following two decades of little net change – the mean spending ratio was 42.6 per cent in 2000 – there was then a rapid increase during the first decade of the 21st century. This took the twelve-country average to 46.6 per cent in 2010. The rise in socialisation ratios was particularly marked in Britain (where the increase was 15.7 percentage points) and the US (8.9 percentage points). Some peripheral euro zone members also went on spending sprees once they were safely ensconced within European Monetary Union (EMU), for example, Spain (plus 7.1 percentage points) and Portugal (plus 9.9 percentage points). Despite the talk of 'cuts', there has been only a modest diminution to a 45.8 per cent average spending ratio last year according to the OECD projections. Government spending in 2013 remained close to its peacetime peaks in many Western countries.

Table 1   **Ratios of general government expenditure, including transfers, to money GDP at market prices (%)**

	1870	1913	1920	1937	1960	1980	2000	2010	2013
Australia	18.3	16.5	19.3	14.8	21.2	34.1	33.9	36.2	35.4
Austria	10.5	17.0	14.7	20.6	35.7	48.1	51.8	52.8	51.8
Belgium	–	13.8	–	21.8	30.3	58.6	49.1	52.5	54.2
Canada	–	–	16.7	25.0	28.6	38.8	40.5	43.3	41.4
France	12.6	17.0	27.6	29.0	34.6	46.1	51.6	56.6	57.0
Germany	10.0	14.8	25.0	34.1	32.4	47.9	45.1	48.0	44.5
Italy	13.7	17.1	30.1	31.1	30.1	42.1	45.8	50.4	51.4
Ireland	–	–	–	–	28.0	48.9	31.2	65.5	42.7
Japan	8.8	8.3	14.8	25.4	17.5	32.0	38.5	40.7	42.9
Netherlands	9.1	9.0	13.5	19.0	33.7	55.2	44.1	51.3	49.2
New Zealand	–	–	24.6	25.3	26.9	38.1	38.1	49.3	43.5
Norway	5.9	9.3	16.0	11.8	29.9	43.8	42.3	45.2	44.8
Spain	–	8.3	9.3	18.4	18.8	32.2	39.2	46.3	43.5
Sweden	5.7	10.4	10.9	16.5	31.0	60.1	55.1	52.4	53.0
Switzerland	16.5	14.0	17.0	24.1	17.2	32.8	35.6	33.9	33.9
UK	9.4	12.7	26.2	30.0	32.2	43.0	34.1	49.8	47.2
US	7.3	7.5	12.1	19.4	27.0	31.4	33.4	42.3	38.7
Average for countries with no missing figures	10.7	12.8	19.9	23.0	28.5	43.1	42.6	46.6	45.8

Sources: Tanzi and Schuknecht (2000) and OECD Economic Outlook (December 2013, Annex Table 25).

Last year, the British government was spending some 2.8 per cent more of GDP than the maximum costs of fighting the 1914–18 war, while President Obama's US government was spending a higher share of US GDP than that recorded during the highpoint of World War II. As a result, numerous Western economies are suffering the strains that our ancestors would have associated only with periods of wartime finance. One reason for endemic budget deficits is that government spending has overshot the upper limit of taxable capacity. This seems to be around 38 per cent of market-price GDP in a typical mature economy.[1]

In response to the associated fiscal strains, many Western governments have adopted the dodges previously only employed in wartime. These include running large deficits, financial repression, forced funding, arbitrary capital imposts – often disguised as regulatory fines – and 'resorting to the printing press', under the name of quantitative easing (QE). The consequent politically induced uncertainty – together with the deficit-induced fear of future tax increases – mean that private businesses have been unwilling to invest, despite high profits and record liquidity. In the context of Grover Norquist's lecture, it is also striking what moderate spenders Mussolini and Hitler were in 1937, compared with their successors. This should give rise to concern. A citizenry without independent resources cannot stand up to a predatory state, especially when that state is also so prominent in the regulatory arena. Indeed, we can see in Figure 1 that the proportion of Britain's national income taken by the government has risen above that taken by the private sector in recent years – a peacetime event with only one precedent.

Where does the money go?

The naive Keynesian emphasis on employing the budget deficit or surplus as an economic 'cure all' has obscured the extent to which the various public expenditure items

---

1   See Sinclair (2012: 64–66) for the evidence.

Figure 1 **Ratios of UK general government expenditure and residual private sector to UK GDP measured at factor cost 1870–2012**

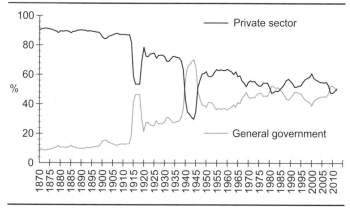

and revenue sources have different effects on the wider economy. The government budget constraint states that all public spending has to be funded either through taxation, the bond market or borrowing from the banking sector. Much of the literature dealing with the effects of government expenditure on the wider economy examines the effects of these alternative forms of finance. However, the consequences of different types of expenditure also differ from each other, even when funded in an identical manner. The international growth literature considered later suggests that public investment in infrastructure, such as transport links, or primary and secondary education can add to a country's growth potential, and are known as 'productive expenditures'. However, these should not be undertaken without appropriate discretion but only if the rate of return exceeds the opportunity cost of allocating the same resources elsewhere, including to output-stimulating tax cuts.[2]

Increased governmental consumption appears to reduce national output, except in the trivial sense that such expenditure is included in the definition of GDP. It is only if GDP increases by more than any given rise in government spending that private-sector activity is stimulated by the extra spending, otherwise private activity – and with it the tax base – will have been crowded out.[3] There appears to be huge confusion about this in the political response to the post-2008 weakness of global activity. The large Keynesian-inspired additions to government consumption since 2008 may have massaged up 'headline' GDP but also exacerbated the downturn in the private sector and led to shrinking tax receipts.[4]

The most damaging public expenditure appears to be paying means-tested welfare benefits to the population of working age. These reduce potential GDP because they reduce the supply of labour to the private sector. The OECD has suggested that only one fifth of government spending falls into the 'productive' category. This means that most public expenditures are 'non-productive'. Non-productive

---

2   This is why political vanity projects such as the HS2 rail link should not be undertaken, even if they are treated as an investment in the national accounts.

3   This refers to the Keynesian multiplier, which has to be greater than unity to avoid crowding out of private activity. This is discussed later.

4   See Young (2013). The title says it all.

expenditures may be used for appropriate purposes but they can be used – and are used – to 'bribe' voters. Such 'public choice' considerations explain why there has been a reduction in government investment ratios in recent decades, despite increased total spending.[5] Norquist's lecture, of course, discussed how to 'neutralise' these public choice pressures and authors of other chapters in this monograph tackle those issues in more detail. Overall, Table 2 reveals that only around one tenth of public spending is accounted for by the two 'primary' government functions of external defence and the maintenance of law and order, corresponding to the Victorian concept of a 'night watchman state'. Even adding in debt interest only brings that total to 8.8 per cent of factor-cost GDP.

On the receipts side, a striking feature of Table 2 is the huge contribution made by income tax and national insurance to the government's revenues with a joint contribution approaching 43 per cent. If the two were combined, no other single tax would approach their importance. Nevertheless, value added tax (VAT) still delivers a significant 16.8 per cent of total receipts. The dominance of a small subset of taxes does not mean that lesser taxes cannot have deleterious second-round effects, if marginal rates are high or the tax is not related to ability to pay. Most economists believe that flat-rate consumption taxes are less distortionary than high marginal rates of income tax. However, the UK tax burden has probably reached the point at which the whole economy is on the wrong side of

---

5 The public choice literature is discussed in Tullock et al. (2000).

Table 2   **March 2013 budget forecasts for UK public spending by function and government receipts in 2013–14**

	(£bn)	(%)	Ratio to GDP at market prices (%)	Ratio to GDP at factor cost (%)
Total managed expenditure (TME)				
Social protection	220	(30.6)	13.8	15.8
Personal social services	31	(4.3)	1.9	2.2
Health	137	(19.0)	8.6	9.9
Transport	21	(2.9)	1.3	1.5
Education	97	(13.5)	6.1	7.0
Defence	40	(5.6)	2.5	2.9
Debt interest	51	(7.1)	3.2	3.7
Industry, agriculture & employment	16	(2.2)	1.0	1.2
Public order & safety	31	(4.3)	1.9	2.2
Housing & environment	23	(3.2)	1.4	1.7
Other	53	(7.4)	3.3	3.8
TME	720	(100.0)	45.1	51.9
Government receipts				
Income tax	155	(25.3)	9.7	11.2
National insurance	107	(17.5)	6.7	7.7
Excise duties	47	(7.7)	2.9	3.4
Corporation tax	39	(6.4)	2.4	2.8
VAT	103	(16.8)	6.5	7.4
Business rates	27	(4.4)	1.7	1.9
Council tax	27	(4.4)	1.7	1.9
Other	107	(17.5)	6.7	7.7
Total receipts	612	(100.0)	38.4	44.1

the aggregate Laffer curve. This means that any attempt to raise taxes makes the public finances worse not better (Smith 2011).

While the structure and rates of tax are important for their influences on the efficient allocation of resources, aggregate supply and economic welfare, budget deficits and taxes appear to have near identical negative 'crowding out' effects on private activity in the long run and similar effects in the short term.[6] This means that the primary problem is the government spending burden and that its financing is a secondary issue. Tax simplification and reform is desirable for reasons of natural justice, reduced compliance costs and increased microeconomic efficiency. However, tax reform in isolation is likely to be of only limited effectiveness once spending ratios are as high as in Britain. Government spending has to be reduced if we are to turn back on the road to serfdom and if we are to restore economic health.

The impact of tax and spending on growth

Deadweight costs

Despite the low government spending ratios prevailing in the late 19th century, there was sufficient concern about the upwards pressure on government spending expected to result from extensions to the franchise for a sophisticated literature on public finance to have developed and for the subject to have split away from the political economy that became modern economics.[7] This early literature anticipated modern public choice theory and gave rise to

---

6 See the statistical equations reported in Smith (2010) and Sinclair (2012: 175–80).

7 See, for example, Bastable (1917), the first edition of which was published in 1892. Bastable's analysis stands up extremely well in the 21st century. Tanzi (2011) discusses the early literature in some detail, concentrating on Bastable's continental European contemporaries.

important concepts, including the deadweight loss of utility that resulted from taxation. These hidden costs mean that taxes impose a burden on society that goes beyond the amount of revenue collected by government.

Such deadweight costs arise because taxes drive a wedge between the price signals perceived by consumers and those received by producers. It is because of the deadweight costs of taxation that flat-rate proportional taxes are considered the least damaging, because they cause minimal distortions at the margin. Most attention has been paid to the issue in the US, where the bulk of the relevant research has been carried out. No British Chancellor has referred to the deadweight costs of taxation within living memory. The likelihood that high marginal rates of tax cause a significant withdrawal of labour hours, and hence high deadweight losses, has been supported by studies that have compared working hours in the US with those in Europe (Prescott 2004) or within the different members of the European Union (Leiner-Killinger et al. 2005). These have usually concluded that countries with a relatively high tax wedge (defined to include social security contributions, payroll taxes, income tax and consumer taxes) on earned incomes tended to record a lower level of annual hours worked per capita.

However, the loss of labour inputs represents only one type of reduction in producer surplus. High rates of tax also lead to a withdrawal of capital formation, enterprise and innovation, particularly where high risk/high reward projects are concerned. The US literature indicates that the deadweight loss represents at least 25 per cent of each additional US dollar of federal income tax revenues. However, this loss can be much greater when the supply and demand responses are high and/or the marginal tax rate is excessive. The deadweight loss associated with a tax increase rises more than proportionally to the increase in the rate of tax.

Supply-side economics

The analytical approach pioneered in the early public finance literature became an intellectual backwater following the Keynesian revolution. However, it then enjoyed a vigorous rebirth with the development of supply-side economics in the mid 1970s (Laffer 2012). Supply-siders applied standard neoclassical microeconomic analysis to the problem of analysing the effects of taxes on the behaviour of private-sector economic agents, particularly with respect to their decisions concerning the location of activity and the timing and levels of their investment and consumption.

A critical implication of the revival of traditional neoclassical concerns by supply-siders is that there are good reasons for believing that the dynamic second-round effects of taxes can be large and rapid, particularly if people anticipate forthcoming tax changes. Once it is accepted that higher taxes reduce aggregate supply as well as demand, many of the accepted ideas for controlling the economy became invalid. Trying to reduce demand through increased taxes becomes inflationary if supply falls by more than demand and not disinflationary, for example.

Furthermore, tax-financed public spending is not neutral in its effects on output, as the demand-based analysis erroneously assumes. This is because of the adverse supply-side effects of increased taxes that result from the reduced incentives to work, invest and take risks. Attempts at fiscal consolidation through raising taxes have different – and notably more malign – consequences than fiscal consolidation through spending cuts. This is now widely accepted in the fiscal stabilisation literature discussed later. However, it was ignored in Mr Osborne's 2010 decisions to raise VAT to 20 per cent and to increase employers' national insurance costs.

Mr Osborne's tax hikes may have been particularly damaging because of the open nature of the UK economy. The spatial consequences of a high tax burden compared with one's trading partners mean the supply of tradable goods moves from high-tax to low-tax economies. If there are no welfare benefits, the former employees in the internationally trading sector of the high-tax economy will seek employment in less productive and less well-paid non-traded domestic services. If benefits are available, the displaced workers from the internationally open sectors will often end up on the dole, particularly if the replacement ratio is too high for the labour market to clear because the government has not allowed for the drop in the market clearing real wage.

This seems to have been one cause of the high UK unemployment in the 1970s and 1980s, particularly in the older industrial regions where living costs were low and productivity was reduced by poor academic attainment. A problem facing all Western economies is that globalisation – and the emergence of Southeast Asian economies where the state spends between 20 per cent and 25 per cent of national output – has speeded up and exacerbated this process. This has hit their industrial heartlands disproportionately hard.

The likelihood that supply is at least as flexible as demand means that supply-side economists have strong reservations about the 'output gap' approach to forecasting inflation, which seems to have largely failed since 2008. The output-gap approach is the forecasting methodology employed by almost all central banks until recently, including the Bank of England.[8] The output gap has also been a crucial element in the projections of the Office for Budget Responsibility (OBR).[9] A changed view about the size of the output gap was a main cause of the dramatic upwards revisions to the projected UK budget deficit between the March 2011 and November 2011 OBR reports, for example.

What does the evidence say?

The mid-1970s 'stagflation', exacerbated by high government spending not only led to the development of

---

8   The Bank now seems to have given up on the output gap, because it is unmeasurable in practice, but has substituted the Labour Force Survey measure of unemployment in its place (Bank of England 2013).

9   The OBR provided an account of its forecasting methods in Office for Budget Responsibility (2011-1 and 2011-2). The role of the output gap was discussed in Pybus (2011). All three papers are on the OBR website.

supply-side economics but also encouraged economists to examine the long-term determinants of growth. This cross-section and panel data literature was summarised in Smith (2006) and Sinclair (2012).[10] Among the findings that have repeatedly emerged in almost four decades of empirical research are the following:

- There is a statistically significant negative impact of increased government consumption on growth.
- Direct public provision of goods and services is more damaging to growth than welfare payments. The government is a poor supplier of goods and services.
- Growth reflects factors other than the government spending ratio. Naive mono-causal explanations should be avoided.
- An increase in the government consumption to GDP ratio crowds out private-sector capital formation almost one-for-one. Economies with high spending ratios become under-capitalised, find it difficult to compete and cease to offer well-paid jobs.
- Inflation is not determined by the spending ratio, as long as central banks do their job properly. This includes recognising when there has been a supply withdrawal and not easing monetary policy when growth slows for supply-side reasons.

Furthermore, quantitatively similar negative coefficients for the effects of government consumption on

---

10 Barro (1997) provides a particularly good account of the issues.

economic growth were regularly discovered. Numerous studies have shown that an extra 1 percentage point increase in the share of government consumption in GDP is associated with a fall of somewhere between 0.1 percentage points and 0.4 percentage points in the growth rate of real GDP per head, with a strong clustering around 0.1–0.2 percentage points.[11]

Competing theories of economic growth

The adverse effects of public spending still may have been underestimated because many researchers employed a 'neoclassical' growth model rather than the competing 'post-neoclassical endogenous growth' approach. Translating the jargon into English, the essential difference is that it is assumed that technical progress proceeds at a consistently steady rate in the neoclassical approach, while the endogenous growth school believes that technical innovation has to be embodied in new capital equipment. Neoclassical theory implies that the level of national output would be adversely affected by excessive government consumption but that future growth would not be once the spending burden stabilised at a particular level. In contrast, endogenous growth theory implies that growth is permanently diminished by a rise in government spending relative to GDP because the technical progress embodied in new private investment will have been crowded out. That means that

---

11 See Sinclair (2012: table 3.4, 133–35) for a tabular summary of three and a half decades of such studies.

Figure 2 **Effect of tax-financed public spending increase in post-neoclassical endogenous growth model**

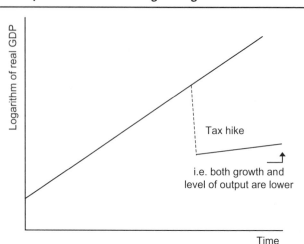

there will be less technical progress if there is more government consumption. Both schools agree that there is a near one-to-one negative relationship between the share of government spending in GDP and the share of private-sector capital formation. The debate is over the consequences of the decline in capital formation on growth.

Figure 2 originally appeared on page 101 of Smith (2006). At the time, it was intended to clarify the implications of the post-neoclassical approach rather than as a forecasting device. Nevertheless, the diagram foreshadows the post-2008 output collapse very well. The extent of the post-2008 output reduction was not expected in 2006. However, given the extent of the rise in government spending, whose effects were then exacerbated by central bank blunders, the fall in growth and, ultimately, output could have been anticipated.[12] As Figure 2 shows, a rise in government spending leads to a lower level of output and then also to a lower growth path from this reduced level of output. This needs emphasising because naive Keynesians appear to have won the political and economic debate, despite the failure of their intellectual frameworks to anticipate the weak output of the late 2000s and the very limited positive response of activity to the massive Keynesian inspired fiscal 'stimuli' implemented in a number of economies.

Furthermore, Figure 3 suggests that the UK's weak performance is because Gordon Brown's re-socialisation of the UK economy led to the phenomenon illustrated in Figure 2. The UK growth trend between 1980 Q1 and 2007 Q2 was 3.26 per cent per annum, while the growth trend from 2009 Q2 to 2013 Q3 was a little under 1.4 per cent per annum. After allowing for the downwards shift in the level of potential output because of the rise in government spending, real non-oil GDP was 0.4 per cent up on its post-2009 Q2 trend by 2013 Q3 but it was 16.6 per cent down on its pre-2007 Q2 trend.[13] Over the whole period from 1980 Q1

---

12 Likewise, the well-known Rahn curve, which shows the government spending burden on the vertical axis and economic growth rate on the horizontal axis, with a growth peak at a government spending ratio of about 25 per cent has never been drawn in such a way that growth actually becomes negative. However, it is entirely compatible with the approach that growth becomes negative if government spending is high enough.

13 The difference between the two explains why people have lost faith in the practicability of the output gap approach.

Figure 3   **UK real non-oil GDP 1997 Q1 to 2013 Q3 seems to reveal a supply withdrawal in practice**

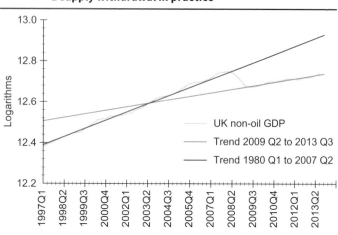

to 2013 Q3 the growth trend was 2.9 per cent per annum, which is much closer to the long-run historic trend. A similar slowdown, from 3–3.5 per cent growth to the 1–1.5 per cent range, was observed in the mid 1970s. It then required the bold reforms of the post-1979 Thatcher government to get growth back on track.

The UK is not unique in apparently having suffered a supply withdrawal. Figure 4 shows the equivalent picture for the entire OECD area. The OECD growth trend between 1980 Q1 and 2007 Q2 was 2.8 per cent per annum, but the growth trend from 2009 Q1 to 2013 Q2 was a little under 2 per cent per annum. OECD real GDP was 0.8 per cent down on its post-crash trend in 2013 Q2 but 12.2 per cent down on its pre-crash trend. A more complex statistical

Figure 4 **OECD real GDP 1997 Q1 to 2013 Q2 also seems to reveal a supply withdrawal**

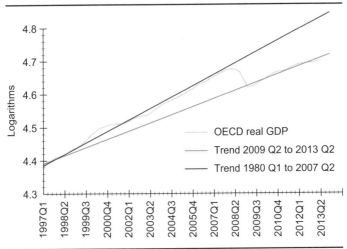

analysis of the determinants of aggregate OECD real GDP over the period 1971 Q1 to 2012 Q3, reported in Smith (2013), suggested that the global financial crash was responsible for only two thirds of the depression in global activity since 2008 while the rise in the government spending ratio between 2000 and its peak in 2010 reduced activity by a further 5.8 per cent. However, this assumes that the financial crash was not itself the result of slower economic growth, which is debatable.

The increase in the British socialisation ratio since 2000 independently suggests that Britain's sustainable growth rate may have fallen by some 2 percentage points during the present century as a result of the large increase in government spending diminishing aggregate supply. Since the values of equities and property represent the net present values of future income streams deflated by the risk-free long-term rate of interest, this slowdown in potential growth should reduce the values of UK shares and property by some 40–45 per cent, all other things being equal. This implies that a tax-and-spend induced supply withdrawal could have been a major cause of the financial crash in Britain. The same applies overseas, where the slowdown in OECD growth theoretically warranted a 29 per cent drop in real asset values (Smith 2013).

In order to illustrate the long-run consequences of the increased size of government over the past half century or so, Table 3 shows the estimated effects of the expanded role of government since 1960 using a 'low-side' estimate of the effect of increased government spending on economic growth of 0.125. The 2013 spending ratios are projected outcomes from the December 2013 OECD Economic Outlook. Spending ratios have been boosted in recent years by the cyclical effects of the global recession. However, government spending ratios peaked in 2009 in the OECD area as a whole and the 2013 figure (41.7 per cent) is identical to the average for the period 2006 to 2013, a comparison that averages out both the boom and the bust.

These figures suggest that anyone who entered the labour force at fifteen in 1960 would have been nearly 3.2 times better off as a sixty-eight-year-old pensioner if government spending ratios had been held at their 1960 levels in the case of the typical OECD country. This invisible opportunity cost of 'big government' arguably outweighs the gains to poorer citizens from policies of wealth redistribution over their lives as a whole, even if the figures concerned should be regarded as illustrative rather than precise.

Impact of government spending and taxation on growth: evidence from econometric models

The use of econometric models to assess policy options did not really commence until the late 1960s, when computers made their estimation and simulation a practical proposition. In the 1970s and 1980s there were heated debates as to whether government expenditure was good or bad for the economy and surrounding the least damaging ways to fund government spending. Unfortunately, the subsequent development of dynamic stochastic general equilibrium (DSGE) models, largely by central banks, has had pernicious consequences because these models tend to assume that output returns to a predetermined trend and have an extremely sparse representation of the government accounts. This means that such models are incapable of simulating the supply-side effects of changes in individual government spending items and tax rates.[14]

This is problematic because simulations using appropriately constructed models still provide the least-bad guide to the second-round effects of tax and spending

---

14 This criticism applies to both the former HM Treasury model now employed by the OBR and the current and previous Bank of England models.

Table 3   **Estimated effects on economic growth of increased public spending between 1960 and 2013**

	Change in government spending burden 1960–2013 (%)	Estimated impact on GDP growth (%)	How much higher output would have been in 2013 with 1960 spending levels (%)
Australia	15.0	–1.9	168
Austria	11.8	–1.5	117
Belgium	24.4	–3.1	392
Canada	11.7	–1.5	116
France	22.9	–2.9	346
Germany	12.2	–1.5	123
Italy	21.8	–2.7	316
Ireland	17.5	–2.2	215
Japan	25.1	–3.1	414
Netherlands	15.4	–1.9	175
New Zealand	10.8	–1.4	104
Norway	15.6	–2.0	178
Spain	25.2	–3.2	417
Sweden	23.3	–2.9	358
Switzerland	20.9	–2.6	292
UK	16.6	–2.1	197
US	7.9	–1.0	68
Mean	17.5	–2.2	214

Notes: Figures in column 1 have been break corrected for definitional and other changes and are not directly comparable with figures that could be derived from Table 1.

changes on the wider economy. The UK policy discussion has become dangerously over-reliant on the purely static calculations employed by bodies whose expertise lies in the microeconomic details of the tax structure. Such static calculations may seriously misjudge the direction, as well as the magnitude, of the effects of tax changes on government borrowing and can give rise to major policy blunders.

One recent UK attempt to undertake a dynamic analysis using a properly specified macroeconomic forecasting model was published by the National Institute of Economic and Social Research (NIESR) shortly after the last general election (Barrel 2010). The NIESR research showed the effect on the level of real GDP of reductions in government borrowing (fiscal tightening) measures equivalent to 1 percentage point of GDP. The government spending cut simulation, for example, suggests that it reduced real GDP by 0.37 percentage points in the first year after its implementation, and 0.14 percentage points in the second year, but that GDP was 0.23 percentage points higher by the third year. Given that government spending is included in the definition of GDP, this means that a 1 percentage point cut in the public spending ratio boosted the residual private-sector component of national output by an amount equivalent to 0.63 per cent of total GDP in year one, 0.86 per cent in year two and 1.23 per cent in year three.

Subsequently, Chapter 2 of Booth (2011) presented simulations of different tax and expenditure assumptions using the author's Beacon Economic Forecasting (BEF) macroeconomic model.

The main findings of this study were as follows:

- The 'best buy' among the counterfactual tax and spending options would have been one in which the VAT and national insurance contribution (payroll tax) increases implemented in 2011 had not taken place but public spending had been cut by a further £20 billion instead.

- The increase in VAT to 20 per cent was a grave error that boosted joblessness by a quarter of a million, cut national output by 1.2 per cent and made government borrowing worse by 0.1–0.2 percentage points of GDP.
- Cuts in government consumption reduced headline GDP but had no immediate adverse effect on private activity while leaving real private domestic expenditure higher in the long run.
- The official UK borrowing projections were far too low. This prediction has been confirmed by the subsequent statistics.

Unfortunately, the complexity and fluidity of the tax system makes it hard to properly incorporate tax measures into an economic modelling framework. This problem implies that the adverse effects of taxes may be understated. It is for this reason that we have to consider the literature on fiscal stabilisation in conjunction with the results from macroeconomic modelling.

However, before moving on, it is worth noting our conclusions insofar as they relate to recent government policy to try to reduce fiscal deficits. The attempt to reduce deficits by increasing taxation leads to lower growth, potentially reduces output and, in addition, may even increase the budget deficit because of the effect on the private-sector tax base. On the other hand, reducing the deficit by reducing government expenditure may well increase private-sector spending even in the short run.

Fiscal stabilisation literature

Organisations such as the International Monetary Fund (IMF), the European Central Bank (ECB) and the European Commission, which have often been required to help bail out fiscally incontinent jurisdictions, developed the fiscal stabilisation literature. This uses a case study approach to see what works in practice and what does not. In this literature, two types of adjustment package are usually identified:

- 'Type 1' fiscal adjustments that implement government expenditure cuts and reductions in transfer payments and government sector wages and employment.
- 'Type 2' adjustments, which mainly rely on tax increases and cuts in government investment.

There seems to be agreement that only Type 1 adjustments achieve a lasting improvement in the budget deficit. This is why it is unfortunate that the coalition government in the UK has attempted a Type 2 retrenchment in practice, while claiming to be implementing a Type 1 adjustment. This has discredited the policies that should have been pursued by tarring them with the predictably adverse consequences of the policies that were actually pursued. There is substantial evidence that Type 1 retrenchments expand output and employment while Type 2 adjustments lead to a worsened budget deficit and reduced economic activity (Alesina and Ardagna 2009). An empirical study by the ECB economists Nickel et al. (2010) into debt reduction programmes in the European Union between 1985 and 2009 came to the following conclusions.

First, major debt reductions are mainly driven by decisive and lasting (rather than timid and short-lived) fiscal consolidation efforts focussed on reducing government expenditure, in particular, cuts in social benefits and public wages. Second, robust real GDP growth also increases the likelihood of a major debt reduction because it helps countries to 'grow their way out' of indebtedness. Third, high debt servicing costs play a disciplinary role strengthened by market forces and require governments to set up credible plans to stop and reverse the increasing debt ratios.[15]

In another paper, the then ECB economists Rother, Schuknecht and Stark (2010) revisited the issue of fiscal sustainability in the light of the euro zone's sovereign debt crisis. The ECB paper argued that the benefits arising from aggressive fiscal consolidation had increased enormously in recent years. Short-term fiscal consolidation was urgently required merely to stabilise the situation, quite independently of the accepted benefits from long-term fiscal consolidation. Specific recommendations were as follows:

---

15 Two earlier papers that came to broadly similar conclusions were the exhaustive study carried out by Turrini (2003) for the European Commission, which looked at all EU fiscal consolidations over the previous three decades, and Schuknecht and Tanzi (2005), who investigated the effects of the cutbacks in the government spending ratios in a number of major economies from the early 1980s to the early 2000s. Smith (2006) summarised a number of other studies that had been published at the time of writing.

- Consolidation should generally be based on government spending cuts, which made such expenditure more efficient, improved incentives to work and demonstrated the political resolve of governments, especially to the bond markets.
- Fiscal reforms should be coupled with structural reforms of social security and financial systems and of labour and product markets in order to maximise the benefits for growth and sustainability.
- The chances of successful and sustained fiscal consolidation could be increased by strengthening the institutional environment for fiscal policy at the national and international level.
- The uncertainty about the magnitude of government liabilities and what constitutes a sustainable fiscal position; the effects of fiscal policy on the economy; the potential self-feeding reactions of financial markets; the risk of a cascade of policy errors, and adverse political-economy incentives, all provided additional reasons for early and determined fiscal consolidation.
- The above factors also suggested a need for extreme caution in any attempt at Keynesian demand management.

In the context of the Hayek lecture, it can be said that the economic evidence suggests that a lower level of government spending increases economic growth in the long term. It is also the case that governments that have high levels of borrowing need not worry about the effects of reducing government borrowing on growth as long as they do not try to reduce borrowing by increasing taxation. Norquist's prescription is therefore precisely correct. Reducing government spending is necessary and desirable. The fact that government borrowing is high is not a good reason to increase taxes and the fact that growth is low is not a good reason to not reduce government spending.

This conclusion is confirmed by examination of the so-called multiplier which measures the impact of (for example) a $1 billion increase in government spending on final national income. The deterioration in the public finances since 2008 has led to new research into the value of the multiplier. Barro and Redlick (2009) examined the multiplier effects of US military spending from 1912 to 2006 using annual data. They typically found estimated multiplier values of around 0.6 to 0.7. This suggests that $300m to $400m of private expenditure was crowded out when exogenous government spending went up by $1 billion. Subsequently, Cwik and Wieland (2010) used five different macroeconomic models with New Keynesian features to investigate whether the post-crash spending packages announced by euro zone governments would boost GDP sufficiently to avoid damaging private activity. They concluded that New Keynesian models did not support the textbook naive Keynesian multiplier claims and the increased spending plans of European governments caused a reduction in private consumption and investment. They also argued that pre-announced future cuts in government spending induced a significant short-run stimulus and a sustained crowding in of private spending.

Even more recently, Ilzetzki et al. (2011) employed a quarterly data set for twenty high-income and twenty-four developing countries to investigate the effect of government expenditure shocks. The main findings were that the output effect of an increase in government consumption was larger in industrial than in developing countries; the fiscal multiplier was zero in countries operating under flexible exchange rates; fiscal multipliers were lower in open economies than in closed ones; and fiscal multipliers in 'high-debt' countries where public debt was over 60 per cent of GDP were zero.

In contrast, Adams and Ganges (2010) found that the multiplier was around 1 to 2 in the case of the US. This may be because the US is a relatively closed economy, as well as reflecting the specific model employed. Another study from the IMF which suggested that fiscal consolidation weakened private demand was Guajardo et al. (2011). Here, the IMF authors employed budget speeches and IMF documents to identify the 'autonomous' element of fiscal consolidation. They claimed that the conventional approach overstated the expansionary effects of fiscal consolidation. However, their methodology may be questionably subjective.

Overall, these studies do not provide convincing evidence for increasing government spending and borrowing to try to increase growth, especially for a country such as the UK given its openness, floating exchange rate and high debt stock. Stimulatory policies that might, just about, work in a large relatively closed economy, such as the US, may seriously backfire in a small open economy, such as the UK.

Conclusion

The rise in the share of national income controlled by the state has been the most important economic development of the past one hundred years. It has had pervasive effects throughout the economies concerned.

Government spending has to be financed through taxes, the bond market or borrowing from the central bank. The upper limit to taxable capacity seems to be around 38 per cent of GDP. As such there should be a constitutional limit on the size of government spending in GDP.[16] If this were set below 40 per cent, the deficit would take care of itself. This limit would be too high to maximise social-welfare or economic growth, but it would, at least, ensure fiscal sustainability.

The growth maximising ratio of general government expenditure in national output appears to be at 20 per cent to 25 per cent, which is where many Asian 'tigers' are currently. Above the 30–35 per cent range, there appear to be no discernible welfare gains from increasing the size of government and the state becomes predatory. Both the US

16 In an important paper the ECB economists Hauptmeier, Sanchez Fuentes and Schuknecht argue that the tension between the tight spending policies in Germany and the big spending policies of many peripheral euro zone members was a major cause of the sovereign debt crisis that followed. The authors suggest that limiting the growth of real government spending to GDP growth less 0.5 per cent looks broadly sensible for countries starting off in reasonable fiscal balance. It would be interesting to see similar calculations for the UK.

and the UK were within that range as recently as 2000 but are now well above it.

The bigger OECD spenders, including Britain, cannot tax their way out of fiscal imbalance because they are on the wrong side of their aggregate Laffer curves. If they try to do so, private activity will slip away, private employment fall, and the budget deficit will widen. Growth falls as the state expands because public consumption crowds out private investment and the scope to introduce new technologies. At the same time, high taxes, the payment of means-tested benefits and increasing government payrolls reduce the labour supply available to the private sector and discourage enterprise.

Excessive taxes and regulations then further reduce the efficiency with which the factors of production are employed. Indeed, the evidence suggests that each 1 percentage point increase in the share of government consumption in GDP is associated with a reduction of 0.1 to 0.2 percentage points in the growth of real GDP per head. Many countries would be far richer if they had held government spending at the levels of half a century ago. Population pressures associated with ageing suggest that the ratios of government spending and borrowing to national output will come under sustained upward pressure.

There is also an increasing problem of citizens' choices not being validly reflected in the political process. This is because there has been a breakdown of the two-way link between taxation and representation with much of the electorate free riding on other people's tax payments.

The work presented in this chapter corroborates Grover Norquist's lecture, both in relation to the necessity of reducing the size of the state but also with regard to the approaches that should be taken to reduce the role of government.

References

Adams, F. G. and Ganges, B. (2010), 'Why hasn't the US economic stimulus been more effective: the debate on tax and expenditure multipliers', *World Economics*, 11(4): 111–30.

Alesina, A. F. and Ardagna, S. (2009), 'Large changes in fiscal policy: taxes versus spending', NBER Working Paper 15438, October 2009.

Bank of England (2013), 'Monetary policy trade-offs and forward guidance', August.

Barrell, R. (2010), 'What are the effects on growth of increases in taxes and cuts in spending?', NIESR Press Release, 18 June.

Barro, R. J. (1997), 'Determinants of economic growth: a cross country empirical study', Cambridge, MA: MIT Press.

Barro, R. J. and Redlick, C. J. (2009), 'Macroeconomic effects from government purchases and taxes', Harvard Discussion Paper, October.

Bastable, C. F. (1917), *Public Finance*, 3rd edn, London: Macmillan.

Booth, P. (2011), *Sharper Axes, Lower Taxes: Big Steps to a Smaller State*, London: Institute of Economic Affairs.

Cwik, T. and Wieland, V. (2010), 'Keynesian government spending multipliers in the euro area', ECB Working Paper Series 1267, November.

De Avila, D. G. and Strauch, R. (2003), 'Public finances and long-term growth in Europe, evidence from a panel data analysis', European Central Bank, Working Paper 246, July.

Feinstein, C. H. (1972), *National Income, Expenditure and Output of the United Kingdom 1855–1965*, Cambridge, UK: Cambridge University Press.

Giudice, G., Turrini, A. and in't Veld, J. (2003), 'Can fiscal consolidations be expansionary in the EU? Ex-post evidence and ex-ante analysis', European Commission Economic Papers 195, December.

Guajardo, J., Leigh, D. and Pescatori, A. (2011), 'Expansionary austerity: new international evidence', IMF Working Paper WP/11/158, July.

Hauptmeier, S., Sanchez Fuentes, J. and Schuknecht, L. (2010), 'Towards expenditure rules and fiscal sanity in the euro area', ECB Working Paper Series 1266, November.

Ilzetzki, E., Mendoza, E. G. and Vegh, C. A. (2011), 'How big (small?) are fiscal multipliers', IMF Working Paper WP/11/52, March.

Laffer, A. (2012), 'The Laffer Curve and the failure of stimulus spending', IEA Current Controversies Paper 38, November.

Leiner-Killinger, N., Madaschi, C. and Ward-Warmedinger, M. (2005), 'Trends and patterns in working time across euro area countries 1970–2004: causes and consequences', European Central Bank Occasional Paper 41, December (www.ecb.int).

Nickel, C., Rother, P. and Zimmermann, L. (2010), 'Major public debt reductions: lessons from the past, lessons for the future', ECB Working Paper Series 1241, September.

Office for Budget Responsibility (2011-1), 'Forecasting the economy', Office for Budget Responsibility Briefing Paper 1, 24 January.

Office for Budget Responsibility (2011-2), 'Forecasting the public finances', Office for Budget Responsibility Briefing Paper 3, 13 October.

Organisation for Economic Co-operation and Development (2013), 'OECD Economic Outlook: December 2013', Paris: OECD.

Prescott, E. C. (2004), 'Why do Americans work so much more than Europeans?', *Federal Reserve Bank of Minneapolis Quarterly Review*, 28(1): 1–13.

Pybus, T. (2011), 'Estimating the UK's historical output gap', Office for Budget Responsibility Working Paper 1, November.

Rother, P., Schuknecht, L. and Stark, J. (2010), 'The benefits of fiscal consolidation in uncharted waters', European Central Bank Occasional Paper Series 121, November.

Schuknecht, L. and Tanzi, V. (2005), *Reforming Public Spending: Great Gain, Little Pain*, London: Politeia.

Sinclair, M. (ed.) (2012), *The Single Income Tax: Final Report of the 2020 Tax Commission*, London: TaxPayers' Alliance and Institute of Directors.

Smith, D. B. (2006), *Living with Leviathan: Public Spending, Taxes and Economic Performance*, London: Institute of Economic Affairs.

Smith, D. B. (2009), 'How should Britain's government spending and tax burdens be measured? A historic perspective on the 2009 budget forecasts', *Economic Affairs*, 29(4): 37–47.

Smith, D. B. (2010), 'Money still matters – the implications of M4X for quantitative easing', *Economic Affairs*, 30(2): 61–67.

Smith, D. B. (2011), 'Restructuring the UK tax system: some dynamic considerations', IEA Discussion Paper 35, March.

Smith, D. B. (2013), 'Financial regulation and the wider economy: unintended consequences', in S. Lawlor (ed.), *The Financial Sector and the UK Economy: The Danger of Over-Regulation*, London: Politeia.

Tanzi, V. and Schuknecht, L. (2000), *Public Spending in the 20th Century: A Global Perspective*, Cambridge, UK: Cambridge University Press.

Tanzi, V. (2011), *Government versus Markets: The Changing Economic Role of the State*, Cambridge, UK: Cambridge University Press.

Tullock, G., Seldon, A. and Brady, G. L. (2000), *Government: Whose Obedient Servant? A Primer in Public Choice*, London: Institute of Economic Affairs.

Turrini, G. G. (2003), 'Can fiscal consolidations be expansionary in the EU? Ex-post evidence and ex-ante analysis', European Commission Economic Paper 195, December.

Young, A. T. (2013), 'Why in the world are we all Keynesians again? The flimsy case for stimulus spending', Cato Institute Policy Analysis 721, 14 February.

4 TAXPAYERS FOR FISCAL DECENTRALISATION

Matthew Sinclair

Fiscal decentralisation leads to better results for taxpayers

In his Hayek lecture, Grover Norquist talked about the importance of the decentralised system of government and taxation in the US creating a process of competition that helps to promote smaller government. Norquist is right. When taxation and spending is less centralised, we should expect that taxpayers will enjoy better results.

Responsiveness

Local government is more responsive to local choices and local needs: it can focus resources on the services that are most valued by the local community; top-down, one-size-fits-all policies set by central government cannot do that.

This chapter draws heavily on work by Mike Denham for the final report of the 2020 Tax Commission: The Single Income Tax.

Cost efficiency

We would expect decentralised government to be more cost efficient because local government can organise its services to reflect costs in different areas much better than central government can.

Incentives

When local government raises its own revenue from local taxes, it has a strong financial incentive to encourage local economic growth. These incentive effects are strongest where authorities are able to set their own tax rates in competition with other authorities.

Accountability

Local government is likely to be more accountable to local people when it is raising its own revenue from local people. People are also more likely to feel entitled to scrutinise the quality of local services.

Experimentation

With many local authorities trying different approaches to delivering public services, it is possible to discover what works much more quickly and cheaply than by relying on top-down direction from Whitehall and better ideas can be copied.

In addition, empowered local government is also likely to attract better quality candidates into local politics, improving the overall direction and management of local public services.

Decentralisation and competition in practice

That is not just empty theory. The opportunity for what Grover Norquist calls a 'U-turn on the road to serfdom' – a chance to reverse the long-term growth in the size of the state – in the United States is the product of a lot of hard work and political ingenuity. The 'leave us alone' coalition that Norquist describes had to be brought together and mobilised. But that coalition was also empowered by the right political institutions. A particularly crucial institution is federalism which he characterises as follows:

> Federalism is: we have 50 states and we want the 50 states to compete to provide the best, most competent government at the lowest cost, to attract people and capital and jobs to stay in their state and move to their state, and we can keep score.

In the United States, the results of that competition are becoming clear. People are voting with their feet and moving from states that maintain big, bloated governments – such as California – to others with leaner governments. Norquist describes how one million people have left that state over the last ten years and statistics on the numbers moving have become so embarrassing that the White

House has tried to stop them from being collected. Indiana is cutting taxes and introducing school choice, Illinois is raising taxes and giving more power to the trade unions and Americans can see the results.

International evidence suggests that the experience in the United States is one that Britain could replicate. The OECD has launched a major cross-country study which for the first time allows us to make proper international comparisons, with their Fiscal Decentralisation Database. The quantitative evidence is still emerging, but the OECD study has already confirmed that local authorities in the United Kingdom have a markedly lower degree of tax autonomy than their counterparts elsewhere. They have the least autonomy in the G7.

A recent research paper from Blöchliger and Campos (2011) at the OECD suggests that the benefits of fiscal decentralisation are part of a more general pattern.

There is a general view that more tax competition leads to more efficiency in the public sector, both by making public providers more responsive to consumers' tastes and by raising the quality and lowering the cost of publicly funded services. Tax autonomy provides voters with an additional lever in shaping the public sector, namely to decide on tax levels, making them more aware of public service outcomes.

The benefits of tax competition go beyond simply providing a local authority's voters with an external yardstick against which to measure performance. Local authorities can also compete with each other to attract households and businesses to locate and pay taxes in their areas. If they are going to prosper and enjoy a growing tax base, local authorities have to offer competitive tax rates.

There is a broad parallel here with the way market competition drives business to be more efficient and offer value for money. Authorities offer a bundle of public services to residents and prospective residents in exchange for a given rate of tax, and the customers choose between them and vote with their feet. Different customers will choose different offers, but whatever they choose, the onus will be on each authority to offer value for money or risk losing them (that is, losing its residents and tax base). That process is not perfect but it is one reason why less centralised public sectors tend to offer better value.

Tax rates are critical to fiscal competition and individual authorities have to ensure their rates are competitive. But, just as with supermarkets, businesses and households will not decide on which local authority they prefer solely on the basis of price. As well as tax rates, they also consider a whole range of other factors, including the quality of local infrastructure and public services.

That means that fiscal decentralisation creates a pressure for local authorities to be efficient, but it does not necessarily create a race to the bottom. Blöchliger and Campos (2011) confirm:

> 'A race to the bottom' cannot be observed. This tends to contradict the view that tax competition may result in taxation levels too low to sustain adequate public service levels.

Fiscal decentralisation instead delivers on two valuable objectives: smaller and more efficient government and stronger economic growth.

Fiscal decentralisation delivers smaller and more efficient government

There has been a long-standing argument in the literature that fiscal decentralisation leads to smaller and more efficient government; studies include Deacon (1979), Mehay (1984), Mehay and Gonzales (1985) and Marlow (1988). Studies using cross-national data have found that more decentralised structures lead to a smaller size of government; these include Cameron (1978), Saunders (1986), Schneider (1986) and Mueller and Stratmann (2003). Decentralisation can only yield its benefits, however, if both responsibility and power are devolved to the local level. Authorities must be free to make their own decisions over both what they spend and how they raise the funds to pay for spending.

On the spending side, the government has already begun to relax restrictions, by reducing the ring-fencing of central government grants for specific programmes. They have made significant progress but Barrow et al. (2010) – a group of successful local authority leaders – have argued they could go much further. However, decentralisation of spending is only one part of the necessary reform programme. To capture the full benefits of decentralisation it is vital local government is also responsible for raising its own revenue.

This then creates electoral accountability. As the Layfield Report (1976) put it:

> [The] first requirement of a financial system for local government is accountability: whoever is responsible for incurring expenditure should also be responsible for raising the necessary revenue.

By making local councils responsible for raising more of their own funds, they are made directly accountable to their own local communities. Financial dependence on local taxpayers means authorities are incentivised to deliver value to their voting customers, rather than ticking boxes laid down by paymasters in Whitehall.

Adam et al. (2008) – in an econometric study from the German CESifo group – look at the effect of fiscal decentralisation on public sector efficiency and studies 21 OECD economies over the period 1970–2000. It concludes:

> Our main finding is that government efficiency increases with the degree of fiscal decentralisation. This result appears to be robust to a number of different specifications and fiscal decentralisation measures.

Specifically, on the basis of the study's main measure of tax decentralisation, the authors find that a 10 percentage point increase in local and regional governments' share of total national tax revenue improves public sector efficiency by around 10 per cent.[1]

---

1 The study estimates that a one percentage point increase in sub-central government's (SCG) own tax revenue as a share of

On that basis, with total government spending in the United Kingdom now at around £700 billion a year, increasing local governments' share of taxes from its current 5 per cent to 15 per cent, for example, would save around £70 billion a year. To put it another way, if we reverted to a system in which our local authorities raised around half their own funding (as they did up to the mid 1960s), the prospective efficiency gains would make it possible to get the same overall standard of public services for around £70 billion a year less than they currently cost.

That figure might sound very high, and it is possible that other differences between centralised and non-centralised countries have led to the study somewhat overstating the scale of the potential efficiency gains, but it does show that there is enormous potential for the decentralisation of Britain's public finances to improve value for money for taxpayers. Indeed, there is considerable scope for increasing savings by making local authorities responsible for running and funding some of the local services currently run by central government. For example, in other countries, local government runs elements of health care and welfare, which in Britain are mostly run by a large number

general government total tax revenue increases public sector efficiency (PSE) by 0.005–0.007 (depending on which of two PSE measures is used). The scaling on the PSE measures is 0–1, with an average of 0.58 for PSE measure 1, and 0.61 for PSE measure 2. So a one percentage point increase in SCG's own tax revenue share improves PSE by approximately 1 per cent. Hence the statement that a 10 percentage point increase in SCG's share of total tax revenue improves public sector efficiency by around 10 per cent.

of quangos that answer to central government. There is a detailed overview of the different agencies at work in Farrugia and O'Connell (2009).

Across the OECD, tax decentralisation is strongly associated with greater public sector efficiency – being able to do more for less.

Fiscal decentralisation delivers stronger economic growth

Gemmell et al., in research for the Spanish Institute for Fiscal Studies, analysed 23 OECD countries over the period 1972–2005, and concluded that:

> economic growth ... has been adversely affected by decentralisation of expenditures but encouraged by revenue decentralisation ... reducing expenditure decentralisation, and simultaneously reducing the fraction which is financed centrally would be growth-enhancing.

The study estimates that increasing the share of local and regional government tax in total national tax revenue by one percentage point increases long-run GDP growth by about 0.06 per cent a year. In contrast, on the spending side, reducing local government's share of spending by one percentage point increases long-run GDP growth by about 0.07 per cent a year.

As the study highlights, these two effects have to be seen together. What the analysis tells us is that when local government spends a lot more than it has to raise in tax for itself, it tends to depress economic growth. Funding from central government grants means that local authorities do not have a strong incentive to grow their own local economy and tax base, and that feeds through directly to lower income growth at the national level.

The study tells us that the worst of all worlds is decentralised spending decisions coupled with centralised tax-raising. Unfortunately, that is precisely the arrangement we currently have in place in the United Kingdom. Local government accounts for around 30 per cent of government spending, but raises only 5 per cent of tax revenues. It is one of the biggest local tax shortfalls anywhere in the OECD.

The Spanish Institute for Fiscal Studies study suggests that narrowing the shortfall could yield considerable economic benefits, reflecting both improvements in public sector efficiency and greater vibrancy in local economies. If local government reverted to its traditional position of raising half its revenue from its own local taxes, we might expect a boost to long-run national income growth of around 0.5 per cent a year, an enormous increase compared with a normal growth rate of around 2 per cent.

Other studies have also found that fiscal decentralisation is associated with higher incomes and stronger economic growth. For example, Buser (2011) measured the impact of fiscal decentralisation on per capita income and found that, in 20 high-income OECD nations, greater decentralisation was associated with higher incomes over the years 1972–2005.

Fiscal decentralisation can be delivered in the United Kingdom

The first thing to note is that fiscal decentralisation here does not require creating new and artificial political units. Britain's existing county, unitary and metropolitan borough councils will work just fine.

Switzerland has a federal system very much like that in the United States. It has a population of around 8 million and 26 cantons, which implies a population of about 300,000 for each canton on average. By contrast, Essex has a population of around 1.4 million (excluding the unitary authorities within its borders) and Hertfordshire has a population of over 1.1 million. Our counties are major administrative units. The unitary authorities are generally smaller but they are hardly tiny. Thurrock Unitary Authority in Essex, for example, has a population of over 150,000. Hammersmith and Fulham Borough in London has a population of over 180,000.

Given that local authorities can and do share services (from waste disposal contracts to chief executives) in order to capture economies of scale where possible, there is no reason to think that they are too small. We should empower our existing local authorities rather than creating new institutions. The 2020 Tax Commission – a joint project of the TaxPayers' Alliance and the Institute of Directors – set out how.

The 2020 Tax Commission – in its final report 'The Single Income Tax' – proposed that at least 50 per cent of all tax-funded expenditure by local authorities should be raised from their own local taxation. That is roughly the historical ratio of self-funding mentioned earlier and it is also the ratio proposed by Chartered Institute of Public Finance and Accountancy, the public finance accountancy body. Over the longer term the ratio could increase further, to 75 per cent or beyond.

The structure of grant funding should also change. Ring-fenced grants should end, so that authorities can decide their own priorities. The taxable base varies considerably between rich and poor areas and needs also vary between areas. Central government has developed a complex system of resource- and needs-based grants to adjust for those differences. In pursuit of equity, the biggest grants go to the poorest areas with the biggest needs.

All developed countries have some form of fiscal equalisation but our system has gone way beyond equalisation, with even the richest authorities getting huge grant allocations to fund needs identified and prescribed by central government.

The figures for England make that clear. According to the Department for Communities and Local Government (2011), taxpayer funding for English local authorities in 2009–10 amounted to £129.3 billion but, of that, just 17 per cent was raised from local taxation. The other 83 per cent came in one way or another from national taxes, via central government grants. Out of the more than 350 local councils in England, well over half were dependent on central government money for more than 90 per cent of their tax funding. Not a single council raised more than 40 per cent of its own tax funding, and only five raised more than 30 per cent.

Equalisation grants undermine the very incentives that are vital to boost local authority efficiency and create a commitment to growth. If authorities can get along on grants from central government, any competitive pressure to provide an efficient service to the local taxpayers who should be seen as their customers comes a distant second.

Under the 2020 Tax Commission proposals, the richest authorities would become largely self-funding. The poorest authorities would continue to receive some support, but on nothing like today's scale. For local authorities to raise 50 per cent of their income would mean decentralising £50 billion of tax revenue, taking local taxes to something like £75 billion annually. That would be around 15 per cent of total national tax revenues – still significantly less than the corresponding percentage in many other countries, including the US, Japan and Switzerland.

Local authorities would lose £50 billion a year of central government grant funding. They would gain new tax powers sufficient to raise at least that amount, but it would be up to each local authority to decide what rates to set for each of its taxes. There would be no requirement for them to stick to the rates previously levied by central government. There are a series of tax powers that a decentralising government could give to local authorities in order to make that possible. In the next section, we discuss those tax powers. There were other taxation powers that the 2020 Tax Commission discussed but then rejected – these options are not discussed below.

Tax raising options for decentralised local government

Council tax

Council tax should remain in place as a practical existing means for councils to generate substantial revenue.

Rates should no longer be capped by central government. Individual authorities should once again be free to impose whatever rate they decide, but fully answerable to their local electorates. They are, and should continue to be, required to hold a referendum on any proposed increase above 2 per cent. Over time, with greater local responsibility, even that should become less necessary.

Business rates

Business rates are another existing and functioning local tax.[2] Until they were centralised in 1990, local business rates were the second major pillar of independent revenue raising for local authorities. They currently raise about £25 billion annually, roughly the same as council tax.

In order to reconnect local authorities with the growth and prosperity of their local economies, it is vital that business rates are once again returned to local control. Local authorities should be free to set their own rate – possibly

---

2 Economic theory suggests that the business rates are a bad form of tax because they apply to a business input, thereby distorting production decisions, which is discussed in Chapter 16 of the Mirrlees Report. The 2020 Tax Commission proposals do not address that broader issue, but equally do not make it any worse.

subject to some upside limit as described below – with valuations determined by the central Valuation Office Agency, as now. Collection of the tax would continue to be in the hands of the local authorities, as it is now, but they would keep the proceeds rather than handing them over to central government.

Tentative steps are already being taken in this direction: from this year onwards individual authorities will be able to keep 50 per cent of the growth in the local revenue from business rates under the business rates retention scheme. But, welcome though that is, it should go much further. Local authorities need to have a direct and substantial revenue stake in local business success.

There is, of course, a common objection. Because businesses do not vote, there is a risk that they will be excessively taxed by local authorities with no regard for the financial health of the companies themselves, and the area's long-term economic future. In the 1970s and 1980s, some 'loony left' councils did exactly that, which was a large part of why the tax was centralised in 1990. That is certainly a legitimate concern, and why some reformers have even proposed the broader introduction of a business vote, as already exists in the City of London. Other ideas include the appointment of Local Business Commissioners to hold councils to account, or Area Growth Boards, with strong business representation and powers over economically important elements of local spending (discussed in Barrow et al. 2010).

There are ways of addressing this concern while still retaining the flexibility for authorities to compete. One idea is that increases in an individual authority's business rate should be limited to the corresponding increase in the council tax rate (although local authorities would be free to set a lower increase – or even a reduction – in their business rate). Over time, the hope and expectation would be that such controls would become unnecessary. Councils and their electorates would come to recognise the benefit of nurturing local businesses.

A second objection is that decentralising business rates would be unfair. Richer councils whose areas host a concentration of businesses would instantly become better off at the expense of poorer ones. And removing business tax revenue from the central pot might not leave enough for central government to redress the balance through equalisation. This was why the Lyons Inquiry (2007) rejected the idea, even though it accepted that 'the nationalisation of business rates in 1990 was not a positive change'.

There is no doubt that decentralising business rates would throw up winners and losers. But simultaneously abolishing the ring-fencing of grants (not proposed by Lyons) would leave plenty in the central pot for equalisation.

Local income tax

A British local income tax (LIT) has been under consideration in one form or another for over a century. In the 1970s the authoritative Layfield Report (1976) concluded it was the only serious possibility for raising more local tax revenue. After re-examining all of the key issues (including administrative costs), even the very cautious Lyons Inquiry agreed that it was indeed a 'viable' option.

Unlike many previous proposals for LIT, the 2020 Tax Commission did not propose it as an addition to the existing income tax, but instead as a replacement for a portion of the national income tax.

LITs are in common use across developed economies, including the leaders when it comes to public sector efficiency: the United States, Japan and Switzerland. So, far from taking a step in the dark, introducing a local income tax here would be bringing us into line with widespread international practice.

LIT has a number of attractions. To start with, it is more buoyant than property tax, allowing local councils to share in economic growth directly, without the need for revaluations or higher tax rates. Local councils are also given a clear and substantial stake in promoting the prosperity of their residents.

LIT is also more progressive than residential property tax, which tends to bear disproportionately on lower-income groups such as pensioners. Used in conjunction with council tax and business rates, it allows councils much greater control over the incidence of their taxes.

The 2020 Tax Commission proposal is that councils should be given the power to levy a local income tax. Their individual rates would be applied at a proportionate rate to all earnings above the personal allowance, with the tax collected by HMRC alongside national income tax and given to the authority. Each income tax payer would then be paying a standard national rate of tax, plus a local tax depending on where he or she lived.

Initially, this would be no more than a simple switch of existing income tax revenue. Instead of funnelling the entire revenue into central government's coffers, a portion would be distributed to local councils. Distribution would be determined by HMRC in line with the residence of individual taxpayers.

At the same time, councils overall would lose an equivalent amount of grant funding from central government. Therefore, the whole exercise would balance financially: local authorities would get more tax revenue but less grant revenue; central government would get less tax revenue but have less to pay out in grants. There would be no overall change for individual taxpayers, at least initially. Overall marginal tax rates would not be higher than the 30 per cent under the 2020 Tax Commission's broader proposals (including national insurance, which would be merged into income tax).

If an LIT were set at an average of around the equivalent of 6 per cent, for example, and the prior national rate were 30 per cent, then the national rate would be reduced to 24 per cent. Individual taxpayers would see their income tax payments split between LIT and national tax, but the overall amount would be unchanged on average.

After the initial creation of the LIT at a certain rate, from the following year, each authority would have power to vary its own local rate annually within an agreed national range. The minimum could be set at zero, allowing authorities maximum scope to compete for new residents with the lowest possible taxes. The maximum could be set at eight pence, giving existing residents, who may find it expensive to move in the short term, some protection against the predations their local council.

Carswell (2004) has criticised proposals for an LIT on the grounds that they are generally not transparent and it would be vital that any LIT was as transparent as possible. For the scheme to generate the right incentives, individual taxpayers would need to know how much they were paying to their local authorities as distinct from what they were paying to central government. It certainly should not be hidden away inside an amorphous total figure.

The 2020 Tax Commission proposed two measures to address this. Those paying the tax via PAYE would have their national and local payments separately identified on their payslips, with a corresponding annual statement for those on self-assessment. Secondly, each local authority would have to provide each of its LIT payers with an annual statement, setting out how much they paid in the previous fiscal year, what rate was charged, how that local rate compared with the national average, and what local rate has been set for the current year. That could be combined with existing council tax statements or new national tax statements currently being introduced.

Local sales tax

Taxes on goods and services (consumption taxes) have often been proposed for decentralisation, for example, in Carswell and Hannan (2008). Other countries, including the United States, have local sales taxes, and there is a good case for Britain following suit.

For one thing, a local sales tax could provide individual authorities with the funding to maintain and improve their town centres, many of which have come under increasing competitive pressure from out-of-town stores. A local sales tax would also give authorities a further incentive to nurture local business, in this case retail business. And in areas with a large amount of tourism, it would give authorities direct compensation for investing to support that industry.

More broadly, there is a strong argument based on fairness, which is that every adult in the community ought to be contributing something to the cost of local services. A sales tax could ensure that. In contrast, council tax only applies to householders, business rates only apply to businesses, and income tax only applies to around 60 per cent of adults. Those problems are discussed in more detail in Carswell (2004).

For these reasons, local authorities should be given the power to raise a new local sales tax of up to 5 per cent on goods and services already subject to VAT at the standard rate, although, for the reasons outlined below, the power would need to be restricted to county councils and large metropolitan authorities.

This new tax would be optional, and not all authorities would choose to deploy it. But it would significantly enhance their fiscal flexibility, allowing them to further shape the incidence of their taxes in the light of local circumstances. For example, an authority keen to attract new businesses to its area might decide to raise its sales tax in order to fund a cut in business rates.

Of course, a local sales tax faces some well-known objections. Firstly, it may be prohibited under the current terms of our EU membership, though this is disputed. Secondly, a local sales tax could run into a serious avoidance problem through cross-border shopping, a problem exacerbated by the growth of internet shopping. Yet although this could be a serious problem, until we try it nobody actually knows. In practice, modest differences in sales tax may not pose much of a problem at all. There is no fundamental reason why authorities offering a convenient and attractive local shopping environment should not be able to make a modest supplementary charge stick. There are already substantial differences in prices across the country, and across different stores, after all. But many people still shop in places such as central London where prices tend to be higher. In the spirit of experimentation mentioned earlier, it is proposed that larger authorities should be able to try a local sales tax if they wish.

Conclusion

There is an important opportunity to secure more responsive politics, more efficient government, a stronger economy and lower taxes by decentralising the UK's public finances. Local governments should not be agencies of central government: they should be the proud municipal governments that have, in the past, played an important role in building great cities such as Birmingham.

We need to end the current farce where, when taxpayers are dissatisfied with poor value for money, local councils and central government just blame each other and no one takes responsibility for improving the situation. There needs to be proper accountability with councils raising the money to pay for their spending priorities.

It is not only in the United States where fiscal decentralisation has been important in reducing the burden of public spending. In Canada, the same thing happened in the early 1990s. Ralph Klein was elected in Alberta in 1993 and delivered sharp cuts in spending, a balanced budget and a flat income tax. There was strong opposition and at one point he said that his 'day was not complete without a protest or two, or three' but voters backed him and his approval rate was 73 per cent in a March 1995 opinion poll after he successfully passed a balanced budget.

In Ontario, Mike Harris launched his 'common sense revolution' in 1995. The three planks of his plan were: cutting taxes and balancing the budget; law and order; and a successful workfare programme. Again the public supported the programme despite fierce opposition and his party (the Progressive Conservatives) was re-elected with an increased plurality of the vote. Indeed, much of the hard work in the fiscal adjustment that rescued Canada from being a fiscal and economic basket case was done by robust provincial governments.

When local government is raising and spending a larger share of public spending, voters can see much more clearly that the money politicians and bureaucrats waste is not just 'public money', it is their money. That tames the special interests driving us down the road to serfdom and makes turning around a lot more practical. Grover Norquist's plan could work in the United Kingdom.

References

Adam, A., Delis, M. D. and Kammas, P. (2008), 'Fiscal decentralization and public sector efficiency: evidence from OECD countries', CESifo Working Paper 2364.

Barrow, C., Greenhalgh, S. and Lister, E. A. (2010), *Magna Carta for Localism*, London: Centre for Policy Studies.

Blöchliger, H. and Pinero Campos, J. M. (2011), 'Tax competition between sub-central governments', Economics Department Working Paper 872, OECD.

Buser, W. (2011), 'The impact of fiscal decentralization on economics performance in high-income OECD nations: an institutional approach', *Public Choice*, 149(1–2): 31–48.

Cameron, D. R. (1978), 'The expansion of the public economy: a comparative analysis', *American Political Science Review*, 72 (December): 1243–61.

Carswell, D. (2004), *Paying for Localism*, London: Adam Smith Institute.

Carswell, D. and Hannan, D. (2008), *The Plan: Twelve Months to renew Britain*, UK: Douglas Carswell.

DCLG (2011), 'Local government financial statistics England', No. 21, London: DCLG.

Deacon, R. T. A. (1978), 'Demand model for the local public sector', *Review of Economics and Statistics*, 60 (May): 184–92.

Farrugia, B. and O'Connell, J. (2009), *ACA-to-YJB, A Guide to the UK Semi-Autonomous Public Bodies*, London: TaxPayers' Alliance.

Gemmell, N., Kneller, R. and Sanz, I. (2009), 'Fiscal decentralization and economic growth in OECD countries: matching spending with revenue decentralization', IEF Working Paper.

Layfield, F. (1976), *Report of the Layfield Committee on Local Government Finance*, London: HMSO.

Lyons, M. (2007), *Inquiry into Local Government*, London: HMSO.

Marlow, M. L. (1988), 'Fiscal decentralization and government size', *Public Choice*, 56(3): 259–69.

Mehay, S. L. (1984), 'The effect of governmental structure on special district expenditures', *Public Choice*, 44(2): 339–48.

Mehay, S. L. and Gonzalez, R. A. (1985), 'Economic incentives under contract supply of local governmental services', *Public Choice*, 46(1): 79–86.

Mueller, D. C. and Stratmann, T. (2003), 'The economic effects of democratic participation', *Journal of Public Economics*, 87(9–10): 2129–55.

Saunders, P. (1986), 'Explaining international differences in public expenditure: an empirical study', paper presented at Conference of Economists, Clayton, Victoria.

Schneider, M. (1986), 'Fragmentation and the growth of local government', *Public Choice*, 48(3): 255–63.

5 FOSTERING A EUROPEAN 'LEAVE US ALONE' COALITION

Nima Sanandaji

In his Hayek lecture Grover Norquist described how interest groups such as families home-schooling their children form a 'leave us alone' coalition in the US. Norquist, who is president of the influential organisation Americans for Tax Reform, argues that the country can move towards increased economic and individual liberty by widening this alliance. This perspective also has clear implications for policy on the other side of the Atlantic. Special interests aimed at increasing the size of the state have long dominated European politics. But the same public choice mechanisms that have encouraged a large public sector can be harnessed, through smart reforms, to foster stakeholders with a vested interest in reducing the size of the state.

Special interests and public sector expansion

It remains a common assumption that welfare states are created through strictly rational and altruistic processes. However, as shown by Warren Samuels and Nobel laureate James Buchanan, one must keep in mind the interplay between self-interest and general interest. According to public choice theory, government policies can indeed be guided by a notion of the common good. But they are also inevitably driven by the agendas of different special interests (Buchanan 1972; Buchanan and Samuels 1975; Samuels 1971, 1972). Dennis Mueller expands upon this idea by noting that governments grow for different reasons. One reason is that governments promise to provide public goods and combat negative externalities. Another is that voters can use governments to distribute income and wealth. A third reason is that interest groups induce government growth (Mueller 1987).

During the nineteenth century, French philosopher and political economist Frédéric Bastiat described how insider groups could use government to restrict free competition. Most famously, in an open letter to the French parliament originally published in 1845, Bastiat demanded that jobs for manufacturers of candles, tapers, lanterns and similar groups be protected by legislation that blocked out the sun (Bastiat 1845). The satirical letter mirrored the arguments used at the time by various groups to protect themselves from foreign and domestic competition. Unfortunately, similar policies still abound, driven not by the notion of the common good but, instead, by those who would use the state to enrich themselves at the expense of others.

The case of the French farmers

In modern democracies, interest groups continue to sway policies in their favour. The result is often that economic liberty and low taxes are traded for state involvement, regulations, publicly funded handouts and burdensome taxes. In France, for example, the farmers' lobby has, over a long time period, through national policy and later also EU policy, been highly successful in promoting public subsidies, trade restrictions and state involvement in the agricultural sector. The result is enormous waste and great inefficiency in the farming market, which hurts foreign farmers as well as consumers and taxpayers.

The main question, however, is not why the farmers support the policies, since the short-term gains of such subsidies are clear. The main question is why such policies thrive in modern democracies when the majority clearly do not benefit from them. After all, most economists and politicians understand the inherent design flaws.

In a paper originally published in 1990 and translated into English the year after, Pierre Coulomb and his co-authors explain why the general interest ends up on the losing side of the farming debate in France (Coulomb et al. 1991):

> French farmers quickly become militant, their demonstrations easily turn to violence; and the farming vote is not to be neglected in presidential, parliamentary or local elections. On the other hand, French consumers and taxpayers do not represent a significant political force. So the tendency of the authorities is, at the least, to avoid confrontation with the farmers: some politicians (Jacques Chirac is a notable example) may actively seek their electoral support.

French farmers are a particularly vocal group, which is more eager than many other similar groups in European democracies to turn to violent demonstrations. However, the mechanisms which explain their political success are basically the same as those of which other special interest groups take advantage. Assume that a thousand European taxpayers pay one euro annually in taxes for supporting a particular group. If one per thousand of the population belongs to this group the total benefit per individual will be a thousand euros annually. The incentives will be strong for those who receive the subsidies to fight to keep or expand them – and, since the subsidies go through the state, to expand the state in the process. The average taxpayer will, however, have little direct interest in engaging in a policy movement to save a single euro annually. Even though subsidies to special interests often reduce long-term efficiency and growth and are often clearly unfair, they can thrive through public choice mechanisms. And since modern democracies contain a range of special interest groups, the total cost for the average citizen can be huge.

Public bureaucrats as a special interest

As brilliantly portrayed in the classic television comedy series *Yes Minister*, public bureaucrats themselves can act as special interests. William Niskanen argues that public employees are budget-maximisers who combine their considerable political power with their direct interest to expand the government sector (thereby creating growth in their own sector) to increase budgets beyond the point of efficiency (Niskanen 1971). Thomas Rower and Howard Rosenthal expand upon this idea, showing that the resulting spending levels are typically higher than those preferred by voters (Romer and Rosenthal 1978, 1979).

It is, of course, possible to counteract the tendencies to spend too much. For this to occur, political parties, tax-payer organisations (such as the TaxPayers' Alliance in the UK or Americans for Tax Reform in the US) or similar groups must gather support for combating government waste. It is, in practice, very difficult to start a policy de-bate regarding each special interest which is enriching itself at the expense of others through the state, but it is possible to address such waste as a general phenomenon. Of course, once support is gathered for such policies, the arduous task of identifying and reforming specific cases must be carried out.

The strong public choice forces pushing for a larger state are thus difficult, but not impossible, to counteract. Not least when taxes and government expenditure reach a sufficiently high level, the costs of the systems become so apparent (as has been the case for several decades in most developed economies) that it becomes possible to create broad support in favour of limiting state expansion or even state size.

That which is seen, and that which is not seen

The situation often becomes much more complicated since state privileges are not always based on taxes and trans-fers. They can also be based on regulations that benefit a group at the expense of society as a whole. A good example is employment protection legislation. Empirical research shows that strict job security laws present a particularly serious obstacle to groups that are often over-represented in structural unemployment, such as immigrants and the youth (Skedinger 2011). In addition, employees in Denmark, with its flexible labour regulations and more limited employment protection laws, still feel more secure in their jobs than do employees in European nations with stricter labour regulations. A likely explanation is that due to a more flexible labour market Danes can more easily find a new job if they lose their current employment.

While labour economists often point to the advantages of labour market deregulation, such changes are nonetheless often strongly opposed by labour unions, who believe that their members – labour market 'insiders' – will suffer from them. By creating rigid labour regulations, the architects of welfare states have created a vested interest. Even when economists point to the great benefits of liberalising the labour market, it will be difficult to convince those whose employment is protected by regulation. The reason is simply that the benefit of such changes – increased labour market dynamism which will occur after reform – is less visible than the existing safety nets that exist before reform. What you have is more visible than what you might gain.

This is in line with another centrepiece of Frédéric Bastiat's ideas: the difference between what you see and what you cannot see. Many of the successful welfare state policies have been built upon the notion that costs should be hidden, and spread out among a large group, while the benefits are to be made visible and preferably concentrated on groups with a strong vested interest in protecting them.

Shifting towards small government

So far we have focused on the difficulties of introducing free-market reforms caused by public choice mechanisms. It is, of course, possible to introduce reforms even though these obstacles exist. For example, more liberal labour regulation can be coupled with welfare safety nets as in Denmark's 'flexicurity' model. After successful reforms the general public gradually can see the benefits to which increased labour market dynamism leads.

In addition, public choice mechanisms do not always favour 'big government' policies. In fact, smart policy can promote support for free-market and 'small government' oriented policies. The core of such reforms is to strengthen various 'leave us alone' coalitions.

If an expansion of government leads to a larger segment of the population being supported through the state, that might in itself create more support for big government policies. But, of course, the opposite might also be true if a larger share of the population gradually becomes supported through the private rather than the public sector. Private firms, their employees and customers can form 'leave us alone' coalitions which support market-oriented policies which, in turn, allow competitive enterprises to flourish.

Voice, exit and loyalty

Today we take competition in television and radio for granted. But many European nations have had state monopolies in these areas for a long period of time. The development of competition in this field is very much in accordance with Albert Hirschman's theory of voice, exit and loyalty (Hirschman 1970).

Faced with government monopolies on broadcasting, many people chose to comply with the regulation (the strategy of loyalty), while some criticised the policies (the strategy of voice) and others chose to circumvent them, in this case by breaking the law and broadcasting privately (the strategy of exit). Those who worked with pirate stations and early private stations, as well as their followers, formed a 'leave us alone' coalition which gathered sympathy from the general public and finally prompted governments to act by allowing competition on the airwaves. Today outrage would follow if governments in Europe were to suggest banning foreign television or radio, or perhaps even returning to full state monopolies.

The 'leave us alone' coalition is so strong in this field that few question it. Governments attempting in various ways to control the Internet today face similar obstacles, which explains why the Internet remains free and full of spontaneous creative order. An important lesson from the development of free broadcasting is that government monopolies sometimes have to be directly challenged by entrepreneurs before real reforms can occur.

Challenging the government monopoly in the provision of welfare services

Sweden has since the early 1990s moved towards a range of free-market reforms. One of those reforms was the adoption of Milton Friedman's notion of providing health care, education, elderly care and other publicly funded welfare services through vouchers. The vouchers follow the individuals and can be spent through either a government or private supplier of the relevant services. Although ideological criticism of the system from parts of the media and from the left is strong, those who choose private alternatives are typically satisfied with their choice.

Reversing the policies towards total state monopolies would go against the interest of the individuals and families who use these services. In addition, opening up public monopolies has allowed many new businesses to be founded. Not least has women's business ownership finally surged.[1] Groups such as teachers and nurses, who previously could only work for government monopolies, can now turn to alternative private businesses and other organisations. This has led parts of even highly politicised labour organisations to support competition.

The Pysslingen revolution

It is noteworthy that the introduction of the voucher system has relied on what Hirschman might have called an

---

1   Nordic nations have for long been, and continue to be, countries with few female business owners although in other respects there is a strong ethic of equal gender values. The reason is that various aspects of Nordic states' government policies, such as public monopolies/oligopolies in the welfare system, hinder business ownership in the sectors in which many women work. Reforms which have opened up public monopolies in welfare have boosted women's business ownership in Sweden (Sanandaji and Lepomäki 2013).

exit strategy. In the 1970s some university students began parental co-operatives for child care, an unusual practice in a time and place dominated by public monopolies. The Swedish Employers' Confederation asked two individuals with policy experience, Bert Levin and Thomas Berglund, to write a book about how private initiatives could go further in order to strengthen publicly funded welfare. The pair, who both had political experience in the Liberal Party of Sweden (a social liberal party) decided, however, that the best course would be to test the idea in reality rather than on paper (Nilsson and Johansson 2011).

Thus the two entrepreneurs replaced the strategy of voice (writing a book) with that of exit (leaving the comfort zone of the system by challenging the state monopoly). The day-care centre formed by the entrepreneurial pair, dubbed 'Pysslingen', needed support from a municipality, since day care is funded through municipalities in Sweden. The municipality of Sollentuna, which forms a part of the Stockholm region, welcomed the initiative. The state, run at the time by a Social Democratic government, had a wholly different attitude. Soon new legislation was implemented to stop the innovative venture. A new law called 'Lex Pysslingen' meant that the state would stop giving financial support to municipalities that opened up the welfare sector to private firms: this could have been the end of the project.

However, Erik Langby, a young politician leading the small municipality of Nacka, which also forms part of the Stockholm region, realised that Pysslingen could continue if it were merely contracted by the municipality to lead the work in a public childcare centre. The private welfare venture could thus survive. In 1991 a centre-right government came to power and formally allowed municipalities to use private firms in the provision of welfare services. Since then, most Swedish municipalities have opened up welfare services to private providers within the frame of public financing.

It is notable that Nacka, with some 90,000 inhabitants, has opened up a number of different activities – ranging from running libraries to local labour market programmes – to voucher systems. The policy has been marked by a desire to experiment, as the municipality has sought out various new forms of activities suitable for voucher systems and attempted to see if they can be reconciled with existing legislation. This small municipality has thus become an experimental workshop for the ideas pioneered by Milton Friedman. The citizens of Nacka have a strong 'leave us alone' attitude, in that they resist both local politicians who want to take away their choice and also state politicians and bureaucrats who desire to meddle with local decisions.

Steps towards more use of markets in welfare

Today health care in the UK is provided through the centrally planned NHS system. Inspiration for change towards a more market-based approach could be drawn not only from Sweden, but also the Netherlands. The Netherlands has created a system where citizens can choose between different private firms which offer them health insurance.

Private companies also compete in provision of the actual health-care services. The system is mandatory, universal and, for those who cannot afford it, funded by taxes. At the same time, individuals are free to pay more to get better insurance.

In both Sweden and the Netherlands, quasi-markets have thus been created in health care in order to combine the political motives of welfare states, such as access to health care for all, with choice and competition. Much can be said about such pseudo-markets, and we need to learn more from experience when it comes to improving such systems. It is, however, clear that these systems have clear advantages over relying solely on health care planned and provided by the state. Even pseudo-markets can, if designed well, promote change and innovation. They can also lead to less direct reliance on the state and create a 'leave us alone' coalition in favour of market-based reform.

If a Swedish-style or Dutch-style health-care system (or an alternative approach that gives rise to more market involvement) can prove successful in the UK or other European nations, it is possible to spread choice and competition to many parts of the welfare state. The result can be citizens that are more dependent on semi-market systems of their choice rather than on fully public monopolistic systems run by the state. Such citizens are less likely to look to the state for solutions to their problems. Perhaps this is not the revolution that some might wish to see but it is a pragmatic step and one that can give rise to productive long-term dynamic effects. This is especially true if consumers of welfare services are allowed to top up the service provided by the state with payments for additional services (for example, paying for comfortable rooms in hospitals or for treatments not funded by the government system).

Privatising pensions

In his lecture Grover Norquist focused on various forms of saving accounts, for education, health, retirement, etc., in order to promote self-reliance and less dependence on the state. One problem with modern welfare state policies is that citizens can become so strongly dependent on a cradle-to-grave system that they make little private provision, reduce their levels of saving and rely too much on state provision in cash or kind. Their destinies are more influenced by the decisions of politicians than by their own decisions. One way to increase self-reliance, and promote a stronger 'leave us alone' mentality, is to reform the existing system so that, for example, individuals are required to save for their own retirement rather than rely on the state for a pension. Citizens would then have less interest in lobbying the state for higher benefits to be paid for by future taxpayers. In addition, they would have a direct interest in a thriving private sector in order to ensure that returns on their retirement savings were maximised. One of the most pernicious aspects of the welfare state is the way in which the current generation of voters is able to obtain promises of future benefits from the government to be paid for by future generations of voters. Individual savings accounts – especially for health and pensions – would reduce this tendency.

Australia is a good role model in this regard. The country has a 'superannuation' system based on mandatory savings and minimum provisions provided by the government for those with low or no incomes. Recently, the Center for Retirement Research at Boston College commented that the system achieves 'high individual saving rates and broad coverage at reasonably low costs to the government' (Kadlec 2013). The UK is moving in the opposite direction. Until 1997, around 90 per cent of the UK working population with workplace pensions were 'contracted out' of part of the state pension scheme and had private provision instead. When it came to the earnings-related part of compulsory pension provision, around twice as many people had private provision as state provision in 1992–93. Successive governments discouraged people from opting out of state pensions and now the option is to be abolished. An important policy reversal, if the UK government is to promote a culture in favour of enterprise, would be in the field of pensions. Private savings should be encouraged as an alternative to state pensions.

'Workfare' not welfare

Australia is also a good role model in other respects. It has long-term experience with market liberalisation and workfare policies. For a long time policies such as trade restrictions, centralised wage negotiations and government intervention in the economy obstructed economic development in Australia. Subsequently, during the 1980s and the 1990s, a wide range of pro-growth policies were implemented, to a great extent by the country's Labour Party. Average labour productivity growth rose from 0.8 per cent in the late 1980s to 2 per cent in the mid 1990s and 3.3 per cent towards the late 1990s. Interestingly, a rising tide did, indeed, raise all ships in Australia – the shift towards freer markets took place without a corresponding rise in income equality. Ann Harding, professor at the University of Canberra, concludes: 'strong economic growth and a continuous fall in unemployment have resulted in private income growth, especially at the bottom end' (Harding 2005).

There are good reasons to replace welfare systems with 'workfare'. Such policies strengthen the social and economic position of families that would otherwise be dependent on the state, as well as fostering growth and making reductions in the tax burden possible because of the different incentives and dynamics that exist within the welfare system. Being able to support oneself is indeed very important in the process of socialising into the role of a responsible adult and, experience suggests, also strongly linked to supporting low taxes, limited government and a market economy. In particular, reforms that strengthen self-employment, as well as ownership of savings, shares and property, aid the formation of strong middle classes with a 'leave us alone' mentality.

Not least it is important to pursue reforms that are effective in creating good opportunities for young individuals to become self-reliant. Reaching fulfilment through individual action is not only at the centre of the modern hipster culture, but also strongly linked overall to formation of political values. Research by Paola Giuliano and Antonio Spilimbergo, who use macroeconomic shocks as a form of natural experiment, shows that young individuals who grow up during times when work is hard to find 'tend to believe that success in life depends more on luck than on effort' and 'support more government redistribution' (Giuliano and Spilimbergo 2009).

Making taxes visible

The last proposed reform relates to the visibility of taxes. In 1903, Italian economist Amilcare Puviani predicted the development of modern welfare states by noting that politicians would hide the cost of the state while drawing attention to its benefits (cited by Baker 1983). This theory has been built upon by James Buchanan and others (Buchanan 1960).

Politicians have introduced fiscal illusion, where tax systems have many small and largely invisible taxes, which tend to be ignored or underestimated by many taxpayers. Modern states are also built upon fiscal obfuscation, where the real incidence of a tax is hidden from the taxpayer. The most obvious example is payroll taxes. These taxes are formally levied on employers but, in reality, mainly affect employee wages and thus have a similar effect to direct taxes on employees. The difference is that payroll taxes are indirect and are largely invisible to employees. Indeed, in general, employees have been shown to fail to identify that payroll taxes are effectively levied on their own wages (Sanandaji and Wallace 2010).

In countries such as Sweden, Finland and Norway, the rise in total taxation since the mid 1960s has been explained fully by the rise in value added tax (also hidden from consumers) and in such payroll taxes. The remaining taxes, including direct taxes on sales and taxes on work which are visible for employees, have not changed as a percentage of GDP. In Germany and the UK, the visible taxes (all taxes except VAT and payroll taxes) have, in fact, fallen as a percentage of GDP, while the rise in hidden taxation has meant that overall levels have risen (Sanandaji 2010).

A vital step towards creating stronger 'leave us alone' coalitions throughout Europe is to work towards making taxes more visible. Individuals and families deserve to know fully how much tax they pay and whether the money goes to justifiable public expenditure that benefits society. Taxpayers' organisations, intellectuals, politicians and others favouring smaller governments should direct their focus on better informing the general public about the cost of government. Perhaps more importantly, the ways in which taxes are levied should be changed to make them more visible.[2] The taxes that are most visible, such as those on property, are those which are most strongly criticised by the general public.

Conclusion

In conclusion, it is possible to foster a 'leave us alone' coalition in European welfare states. Issues such as religious

---

2 For example, by replacing employers' taxes with income taxes.

freedom and home-schooling that Grover Norquist explains are important in the US are also relevant in parts of Europe. But, as Norquist himself notes, significant cultural differences exist between Europe and the US, which means that these issues are of less significance in Europe. Differences, of course, also exist within Europe. However, the overall changes that can strengthen 'leave us alone' coalitions are arguably similar across Europe. Market reforms can increase the appetite for further market reforms and create a virtuous circle characterised by a strengthening of the private sector, the promotion of individual self-reliance, increasing choice and competition within welfare systems and, finally, making taxes and other costs of government more visible. Such reforms can hopefully not only benefit society directly but also lower the 'reform-threshold', making future reforms easier to implement.[3]

References

Baker, S. H. (1983), 'The determinants of median voter tax liability: an empirical test of the fiscal illusion hypothesis', *Public Finance Quarterly*, 11(1): 95–108.

Bastiat, F. (1845), 'The candlemakers' petition – an economic fable', reprinted by Silent Partner Consulting (2001), *Policy*, 17(2).

---

3 The idea of a 'reform threshold' is a central theme in *Renaissance for Reforms*, a book co-authored by Nima Sanandaji and Professor Stefan Fölster, and published by Timbro in association with the Institute of Economic Affairs.

Buchanan, J. (1960), *Fiscal Theory and Political Economy*, Chapel Hill, NC: University of North Carolina Press.

Buchanan, J. (1972), 'Politics, property, and the law: an alternative interpretation of Miller et al v. Schoene', *Journal of Law and Economics*, 15(2): 439–52.

Buchanan, J. and Samuels, W. (1975), 'On some fundamental issues in political economy: an exchange of correspondence', *Journal of Economic Issues*, 9(1): 15–38.

Coulomb, P., Delorme, H., Hervieu, B., Jollivet, M. and Lacombe, P. (1991), *Farmers and Politics in France*, Streatley, UK: The Arkleton Trust.

Giuliano, P. and Spilimbergo, A. (2009), 'Growing up in a recession: beliefs and the macroeconomy', IZA Discussion Paper 4365.

Harding, A. (2005), 'Recent trends in income inequality in Australia', presentation at Sustaining Prosperity: New Reform Opportunities for Australia, Melbourne, Australia, 31 May.

Hirschman, A. O. (1970), *Exit, Voice, and Loyalty: Responses to Decline in Firms, Organizations, and States*, Cambridge, MA: Harvard University Press.

Kadlec, D. (2013), 'Mandatory savings: how Australia fixed a retirement crisis', *Time*, 22 April.

Mueller, D. (1987), 'The growth of government: a public choice perspective', staff paper, *International Monetary Fund*, 34(1): 115–49.

Nilsson, M. and Johansson, O. (2011), *Mångfald eller enfald? Framtiden efter friskolereformen*, Stockholm, Sweden: Sektor3 and Timbro.

Niskanen, W. (1971), *Bureaucracy and Representative Government*, Chicago, MI: Aldine-Atherton.

Romer, T. and Rosenthal, H. (1978), 'Political resource allocation, controlled agendas, and the status quo', *Public Choice*, 33: 27–43.

Romer, T. and Rosenthal, H. (1979), 'Bureaucrats versus voters: on the political economy of resource allocation by direct democracy', *Quarterly Journal of Economics*, 93: 563–87.

Samuels, W. (1971), 'Interrelations between legal and economic process', *Journal of Law and Economics*, 14(2): 435–50.

Samuels, W. (1972), 'In defense of a positive approach to government as an economic variable', *Journal of Law and Economics*, 15(2): 453–59.

Sanandaji, N. (2010), 'Dolda skatter i fokus', Swedish Federation of Business Owners.

Sanandaji, N. and Lepomäki, E. (2013), 'The lack of female entrepreneurs in Nordic welfare states', Brussels: Libera.

Sanandaji, T. and Wallace, B. (2010), 'Fiscal illusion and fiscal obfuscation: an empirical study of tax perception in Sweden', Research Institute of Industrial Economics (IFN), IFN Working Paper 837.

Skedinger, P. (2011), 'Employment consequences of employment protection legislation', Research Institute of Industrial Economics (IFN), IFN Working Paper 865.

ABOUT THE IEA

The Institute is a research and educational charity (No. CC 235 351), limited by guarantee. Its mission is to improve understanding of the fundamental institutions of a free society by analysing and expounding the role of markets in solving economic and social problems.

The IEA achieves its mission by:

- a high-quality publishing programme
- conferences, seminars, lectures and other events
- outreach to school and college students
- brokering media introductions and appearances

The IEA, which was established in 1955 by the late Sir Antony Fisher, is an educational charity, not a political organisation. It is independent of any political party or group and does not carry on activities intended to affect support for any political party or candidate in any election or referendum, or at any other time. It is financed by sales of publications, conference fees and voluntary donations.

In addition to its main series of publications the IEA also publishes a quarterly journal, *Economic Affairs*.

The IEA is aided in its work by a distinguished international Academic Advisory Council and an eminent panel of Honorary Fellows. Together with other academics, they review prospective IEA publications, their comments being passed on anonymously to authors. All IEA papers are therefore subject to the same rigorous independent refereeing process as used by leading academic journals.

IEA publications enjoy widespread classroom use and course adoptions in schools and universities. They are also sold throughout the world and often translated/reprinted.

Since 1974 the IEA has helped to create a worldwide network of 100 similar institutions in over 70 countries. They are all independent but share the IEA's mission.

Views expressed in the IEA's publications are those of the authors, not those of the Institute (which has no corporate view), its Managing Trustees, Academic Advisory Council members or senior staff.

Members of the Institute's Academic Advisory Council, Honorary Fellows, Trustees and Staff are listed on the following page.

The Institute gratefully acknowledges financial support for its publications programme and other work from a generous benefaction by the late Alec and Beryl Warren.

Other papers recently published by the IEA include:

Taxation and Red Tape
The Cost to British Business of Complying with the UK Tax System
Francis Chittenden, Hilary Foster & Brian Sloan
Research Monograph 64; ISBN 978-0-255-36612-0; £12.50

Ludwig von Mises – A Primer
Eamonn Butler
Occasional Paper 143; ISBN 978-0-255-36629-8; £7.50

Does Britain Need a Financial Regulator?
Statutory Regulation, Private Regulation and Financial Markets
Terry Arthur & Philip Booth
Hobart Paper 169; ISBN 978-0-255-36593-2; £12.50

Hayek's The Constitution of Liberty
An Account of Its Argument
Eugene F. Miller
Occasional Paper 144; ISBN 978-0-255-36637-3; £12.50

Fair Trade Without the Froth
A Dispassionate Economic Analysis of 'Fair Trade'
Sushil Mohan
Hobart Paper 170; ISBN 978-0-255-36645-8; £10.00

A New Understanding of Poverty
Poverty Measurement and Policy Implications
Kristian Niemietz
Research Monograph 65; ISBN 978-0-255-36638-0; £12.50

The Challenge of Immigration
A Radical Solution
Gary S. Becker
Occasional Paper 145; ISBN 978-0-255-36613-7; £7.50

Sharper Axes, Lower Taxes
Big Steps to a Smaller State
Edited by Philip Booth
Hobart Paperback 38; ISBN 978-0-255-36648-9; £12.50

Self-employment, Small Firms and Enterprise
Peter Urwin
Research Monograph 66; ISBN 978-0-255-36610-6; £12.50

Crises of Governments
The Ongoing Global Financial Crisis and Recession
Robert Barro
Occasional Paper 146; ISBN 978-0-255-36657-1; £7.50

Other IEA publications

Comprehensive information on other publications and the wider work of the IEA can be found at www.iea.org.uk. To order any publication please see below.

Personal customers

Orders from personal customers should be directed to the IEA:

Clare Rusbridge
IEA
2 Lord North Street
FREEPOST LON10168
London SW1P 3YZ
Tel: 020 7799 8907. Fax: 020 7799 2137
Email: sales@iea.org.uk

Trade customers

All orders from the book trade should be directed to the IEA's distributor:

NBN International (IEA Orders)
Orders Dept.
NBN International
10 Thornbury Road
Plymouth PL6 7PP
Tel: 01752 202301, Fax: 01752 202333
Email: orders@nbninternational.com

IEA subscriptions

The IEA also offers a subscription service to its publications. For a single annual payment (currently £42.00 in the UK), subscribers receive every monograph the IEA publishes. For more information please contact:

Clare Rusbridge
Subscriptions
IEA
2 Lord North Street
FREEPOST LON10168
London SW1P 3YZ
Tel: 020 7799 8907, Fax: 020 7799 2137
Email: crusbridge@iea.org.uk